PRAISE FOR *GIRLS*

"As a youth star herself, Melody provides a great and inspirин̴ᵣᵣᵢₑ tive that all youth athletes can learn from. I enjoyed the book and her story. Thanks for sharing your journey!"

—JORDAN HASAY, PROFESSIONAL AMERICAN RUNNER

"*Girls Running* is a very timely book for young women and girls who want to make running a healthy, fun, and meaningful part of their lives. The book provides a great balance of information regarding training, nutrition, mindfulness, and both physical and mental exercises for young and engaged minds."

—JOAN BENOIT SAMUELSON, FIRST WOMEN'S OLYMPIC MARATHON CHAMPION

"*Girls Running* gives young athletes a perspective into how to achieve long-term success and happiness by covering a wide range of topics such as how to fuel properly, have a positive body image, be a team player, and have a growth mindset."

—KARISSA SCHWEIZER, AMERICAN MIDDLE- AND LONG-DISTANCE RUNNER

"It didn't take long into reading *Girls Running* to realize how much I wish I had been introduced to this book as a young athlete, and how so many aspects resonate with me now as a professional athlete. It's all-encompassing with the information it provides on both the physical and mental realm of running, while also providing moments for reflection to process the information on a personal level. A fantastically informative and relatable read no matter what part of your journey as a runner (or triathlete) you are on."

—KATIE ZAFERES, 2016 OLYMPIAN, WORLD CHAMPION, AND PROFESSIONAL TRIATHLETE

"*Girls Running* is the perfect guide for young female runners at any level to learn how to make the most of the running journey. From nutrition, to the mental side of competition, to celebrating all the female body can do, this book is a resource all young athletes should have."

—COURTNEY FRERICHS, OLYMPIC STEEPLECHASER

"I wish I had this amazing book when I was younger, but the next best thing is getting to read it now. *Girls Running* deftly weaves together stories and lessons for female athletes, simultaneously lifting me up and lighting my fire. The book empowers me as a coach, athlete, and human."

—MEGAN ROCHE, MD, PRO RUNNER, AND COACH

GIRLS RUNNING

ALL YOU NEED TO STRIVE, THRIVE, AND RUN YOUR BEST

Melody Fairchild
& Elizabeth Carey

VELO.
press

Boulder, Colorado

4745 Walnut Street, Unit A
Boulder, CO 80301–2587 USA

VeloPress is the leading publisher of books on endurance sports and is a division of Pocket Outdoor Media. Focused on cycling, triathlon, running, swimming, and nutrition/diet, VeloPress books help athletes achieve their goals of going faster and farther. Preview books and contact us at velopress.com.

Distributed by Ingram Publisher Services

Library of Congress Cataloging-in-Publication Data

Names: Fairchild, Melody, author. | Carey, Elizabeth, author.
Title: Girls running: All you need to strive, thrive, and run your best /
    Melody Fairchild and Elizabeth Carey.
Description: Boulder, Colorado: VeloPress, 2020. | Includes
    bibliographical references. | Audience: Ages 12–18 | Audience: Grades
    10–12 |
Identifiers: LCCN 2020013488 (print) | LCCN 2020013489 (ebook) | ISBN
    9781948007184 (paperback) | ISBN 9781948006286 (ebook)
Subjects: LCSH: Running for girls—Juvenile literature.
Classification: LCC GV1061.18.G47 F35 2020 (print) | LCC GV1061.18.G47
    (ebook) | DDC 796.42082—dc23
LC record available at https://lccn.loc.gov/2020013488
LC ebook record available at https://lccn.loc.gov/2020013489

This paper meets the requirements of ANSI/NISO Z39.48-1992 (Permanence of Paper).

Art direction and interior design by Vicki Hopewell
Cover and interior illustrations by Åsa Gilland
Photography by Glen Delman, p. 221, and Jess Barnard, p. 222

20 21 22 / 10 9 8 7 6 5 4 3 2 1

*To all girls. May this book inspire a running journey
guided by a self-love so great that nothing can stop you.*

CONTENTS

Introduction xi

1 Your Running Journey 1
How to embrace your own path
Melody's journey
Role models

2 Hello, Body! 11
A run through the systems that keep you moving
Body parts and systems
Heart rate
Puberty and periods 101

3 Train like a Boss 29
The magic of work and rest
Running form
Recovery and sleep tips
Strength, core, and mobility routines
Crosstraining workouts

4 Adaptations 55
Zoom in on progress and growth
Running systems and why you do specific workouts
Periodizing your season and career
Pain and sickness
Training logs

5   Running with Hormones...................................71
How to train and race your best through puberty and periods
Puberty for athletes
Periods and their phases decoded, plus tips for dealing

6   A Winning Mindset 85
Yes, you can handle pressure and meet your goals
Intro to mindfulness
Goal setting
Sports psychology tools, including visualization
Mental health and when to get help

THE JOURNEY OF WOMEN'S RUNNING: A TIMELINE 103

7   Compete like a Champion 109
Tips and strategies for racing fierce
Pacing yourself
Teamwork and scoring
Overcoming challenges
Running in college

8   Fueling for Success....................................125
How to feed yourself and your busy life
Sports nutrition and energy balance
What to eat—plus why and when
Hunger signs
Special diets
Recipes

9 Food & Body Issues 153
How to tackle problems head-on

Body shaming
Racing weight and other myths
Dangers of underfueling, including Relative Energy Deficiency
   in Sport (RED-S)
Disordered eating, body issues, and when to get help

10 Building a Great Team 173
It takes a village, and these are the people you want in it

Intuition and discernment
Building your support crew
How to find doctors, PTs, RDs, and other experts (and what to ask them)
Being a good teammate

11 Gearing Up 195
The basics and the extras

Sports bras
Running shoes and spikes
Other gear

Acknowledgments 211

Selected Bibliography 213

About the Authors 221

INTRODUCTION

Running is the best. Commit to it, and it delivers. Think: endurance, speed, wind in your hair, competition, lifelong friends, and unforgettable experiences. It doesn't always come easy though. That's where we come in.

This guide will empower you to pursue a healthy, happy, successful relationship with running. Inspired by Melody Fairchild's journey and buoyed by science, research, and interviews with experts and athletes, this book offers guidance, insights, and tools so you can make the most of your running experience. We share revelations and lessons learned after more than 100,000 combined lifetime miles and six decades as athletes and coaches. The information in here is inspired by real questions we've heard time and time again, from coaches, parents, and runners like you.

Entire professions are devoted to each subject we explore—they're important. We can't go into that depth of detail in this book. But what we can do is share key information that we hope enlightens your own next steps.

Each chapter includes writing prompts. These are invitations for you to dive deeper into your own journey. There's no right way to write. Think of the prompts as blank, safe spaces for you to reflect on running and beyond. To write, find a quiet, comfortable place to sit. Silence your phone and inner critic. Choose a prompt, set a timer, and then write, ideally on paper. Don't worry about grammar or making sense; keep moving your pen or pencil and go where it takes you.

This guide is a lot of things. It's a toolkit, so when it feels like things are falling apart—and let's be honest, that happens to all of us!—you've got tools that will help you put them back together. This is also a launchpad with invitations to help you surge forward as you grow in your running and in your life. Finally, it's a resource to help us all run stronger, faster, and smarter together.

In this book, we'll use the words *female*, *girls*, and *women* and discuss binary sports divisions, but we welcome all readers. Most of all, we're grateful that you're here.

Ready? Let's go!

1

YOUR RUNNING JOURNEY

HOW TO EMBRACE YOUR OWN PATH

Melody was set to race on a flat indoor track in snowy Syracuse, New York, at the national championships. At the sound of the starter's pistol, girls shot off the line in the 2-mile race. Melody let them sprint ahead, reminding herself of her plan. *I am the best runner here. It's me against the clock*, she thought, channeling confidence. *Run with a clear mind—no distractions, no doubt.*

Like an airplane picking up speed on the ground before liftoff, she soon sailed past the others, soaring into the lead. She heard her coach yelling splits. A mile in, he shouted, "5:03! Behind! Pick it up!" His yell shot adrenaline through her, and she surged farther ahead. In the second mile, she felt like a bull charging, red-hot with anger at even the thought of failure. She lapped girls, forced to swing wide into the second lane.

The bell rang, signaling the final lap. Another shot of adrenaline coursed through her. She knew she was under record pace but dug deeper to make a lasting mark. And she did, running 9:55.92. She was the first US high school girl to run faster than 10 minutes for the 2-mile. En route, she also set the indoor 3,000-meter record: 9:17.07.

That record-setting 2-mile race in 1991 was just one step in Melody's running journey. Inspired by a fire in her belly, her journey became about more than winning races; you'll hear about that in this chapter. We'll look at how you can shape your own running journey into a wonderful, wild adventure inspired by curiosity, hard work, and the fire in your own belly. You'll also meet other athletes who use their running journeys to make a difference both in and beyond sport.

MELODY'S JOURNEY

From the start, Melody loved running and excelled at racing. When she was 9 years old, she ran up a steep canyon near her home to see how fast she could do it.

> One day I announced to my family, "I'm running to the house-behind-the-rock." I don't know if anyone was actually listening. But I didn't hear anyone say, "You can't," or "It's not safe," or "Why would you want to do that?" I recall a twinkly eyed smile from my father, which was all the acknowledgment I needed. I hopped out the door of our home in Boulder, Colorado, and summoned up the courage to venture into the great unknown. The butterflies fluttered within me. How would my body respond? I crossed a single-lane bridge over the creek, turned my nose up-canyon, and said, "Let's go."
>
> I reached the house-behind-the-rock in about a minute. While I'd held that place in my imagination in a cloud of mystery and intrigue, it was actually just a mere 200 meters away from our doorstep. I smiled and said, "Hah!" I felt satisfaction.
>
> Completing that mission birthed another desire. I grabbed a stick and etched a deep line in the dirt shoulder of the road that wound through the canyon. "I will go one step farther next time," I said. Each

time I ran to the line, I added a step. Soon five steps then 100 steps. Each time I ran, I wanted the canyon to carve a path in my soul, which would bring me closer to myself. As an elementary school kid, I ran 2.5 miles up and 2.5 miles down, racing the hands of the grandfather clock at home, checking to see if I had come a little closer to my essence through pure effort and speed. —**MELODY FAIRCHILD**

At 10, Melody earned her first age-group win in the 10K. In middle school, she set the 1600-meter school record: 5:25. At 14, she raced at her first high school cross-country meet. Before that race, she was so nervous she thought of purposely missing the bus. She didn't. Instead, she competed with her team and won the 5K event.

Melody loved competition and to win. She had a crystal-clear vision of herself as a champion. But her motivation came from within, pushing her to race the clock, herself, and her competitors, always with a singular, close-up intensity that blurred everything else out of focus.

She trained with her teammates in Boulder, Colorado, but also spent a lot of time running alone. Running transcended life at home, where her mother was sick with cancer and her father's alcoholism had driven his business into the ground, leaving the family in dire straits financially.

In high school, Melody won eight state championship titles in cross country and track and field in total. She set state records in cross country (16:45.1 for 5K) and on the track in the 1600 meters (4:49.86) and 3200 meters (10:34.0), all at about a mile above sea level. As a junior, she won the sole US high school cross-country championships (now called Foot Locker). She defended her title the following year, setting a course record (16:39) that still stands. That same year, as a senior in high school, she broke the 2-mile record in Syracuse and earned bronze at the IAAF World Junior Cross Country Championships in Antwerp, Belgium.

With a resume like hers, Melody received a lot of attention from colleges. She selected the University of Oregon, where the team culture felt welcoming.

The transition to college was difficult. Two months prior, Melody held her mother's hand as she took her last breath. "In that moment, I was thrust into the unknown," Melody says. In the unknown, she faced fear and darkness. She felt lost. Melody had won nearly every race she'd entered, but had yet to encounter a sidelining setback, let alone the deep uncharted waters of grief.

Melody's grief, coupled with burnout and injury, kept her from racing with the Ducks during her freshman year. She qualified for the World Cross Country Championships but was reinjured and could not race. Heartbroken, she decided to listen to the advice her mother had given her the year before: Take a year off.

She returned to Colorado, stopped running, and supported herself by working several jobs. As she recuperated, her hormones flowed, and she—finally!—got her period. Although she had feared it, that rite of passage brought her hope. She strength trained intensively. She made new friends and started to laugh again. Eventually she returned to running, jaunting to mountaintops and feeling out her goals.

Never had I thought as a top high school runner that to be a champion I had to embrace my vulnerabilities, to try and fail and try again. I didn't have to be perfect. To expect to continue to win, without intermission, was insanity. In this way, the trauma of losing my mother was a blessing. It sent me hurtling into a territory so vast that I spent many a night my freshman year sitting in bed in my single dorm room feeling totally disoriented. These times are essential for becoming. They are when we find out who we are. —M.F.

After a year off, she returned to the University of Oregon, where she embraced new challenges with an open mind. She learned to duke it out with the back of the pack, rather than race from the front. She trained patiently, with a newfound sense of playfulness and community. She befriended her teammates and took on a leadership role, helping the Ducks finish fifth at the NCAA cross-country championships, when she earned her first All-American honor. The diligence paid off, in particular when she won a national title in the indoor 3,000-meter race, running 9:07 and surpassing the times she ran in high school.

After college, Melody became a professional runner, qualifying for the US Olympic Trials in the 10K and marathon and making the US World Track and Field Championships team. She found additional success as a masters competitor and also on the trails, racing at the World Mountain Running Championships.

Today, Melody continues to enjoy the challenge of embracing the unknown. Since turning 40, she's won five US titles and given birth to her son, Dakota, the greatest joy of her life.

As both an athlete and coach, Melody's goal is to inspire people to get out there. She directs a year-round youth running program, coaches a women's training group, and founded a girls' running camp, all with the aim of creating space for others' running journeys to flourish.

What beckoned Melody? Above all, adventure! Curiosity piqued, she embarked—not knowing that her more-than-61,000-mile journey would include darkness along with light, and continual discovery of her authentic self and passion.

YOUR RUNNING JOURNEY: START HERE

Whether you yet feel it, there's a flame flickering within you. Stoke it and it'll turn into a "fire in your belly." It's your guide as you travel from the known into the unknown and back again. It's your intuition, ignited by passion and transformed into action in the world by strength of resolve. It'll be with you as you run into and through obstacles throughout your journey. As you'll see, the running journey empowers us to elevate our families, our communities, and our world.

The running journey starts in your comfort zone. Then desire beckons, as it did to Melody looking up the hill from her house. You might waffle: Should I go?

When you commit to taking those first steps forward, you enter the unknown. It's here you face fears. It's here you hear the excuse-maker. It's here you learn to strengthen your grit muscles and callous your skin. It's here you hone your patience. It's here you begin to learn who you are and all that you can become.

The running journey is not for the faint of heart. Sure, you could stay safe in your comfort zone. But being your best self means stepping into the unknown and its new experiences. If you have inklings of dreams in your heart to be or to do more, they require you to grow. All of us were born with unlimited potential, but we must be willing to take risks to reach it. That means sometimes we fall short. And then we try again.

Running invites us to practice for our longest race—life! It is made up of countless mini-running journeys. Cross country and track and field, for example, are ripe for trying, testing, and growing. The team environment allows you to develop as an individual while also contributing to a community. You're essential to fellow adventure-seekers.

Does the journey feel scary and uncomfortable? Yep! It takes guts, especially to try new things, miss goals, or "fail." But know this: Your journey hinges on the attempt, not the end result. Medals are nice and shiny, but running is most potent when it is about more than prizes. Stick with it and you'll see—the process of running opens doors to new places and greater understanding time and again.

RUNNING JOURNEYS INSPIRING CHANGE

The running journey inspires us to achieve incredible feats. Sometimes those feats land us on a podium, and sometimes they carry us far beyond the bright lights. In fact, the running journey inspires some runners to become ambassadors for change. Whether advocating for the environment or marginalized people, raising money for scientific research, calling out sponsors for discrimination, or encouraging body positivity, these athletes elevate our sport and motivate the world around them.

Here is a closer look at eight running role models.

Alysia Montaño (Olympian, world championship medalist, national champ, and American record-setting middle-distance runner), Allyson Felix (Olympic champion and track athlete with the most world championship gold medals: 13!), and Kara Goucher (Olympian and silver medalist at the world champs) all spoke out about Nike, a powerful sponsor, and its treatment of pregnant athletes. They've inspired new sponsorships that include maternity protection.

Jordan Marie Brings Three White Horses Daniel, member of the Kul Wicasa Oyate/Lower Brule Sioux tribe, races as an advocate of indigenous people, who are often mis- and underrepresented. She has raced with a red hand painted across her mouth to bring awareness to and pray for Missing and Murdered Indigenous Women. If you are passionate about changing something, she says, stand up for yourself and others. She says it can be as simple as wearing a pin: "The smallest things can lead to the biggest outcomes."

Gabriele Grunewald was a top US middle-distance runner who died of cancer at age 32. Despite her diagnosis and challenging treatments, she continued running and chasing dreams, even in the face of fear. She shared her journey with the world, using her platform to raise awareness for cancer patients and founding Brave Like Gabe, a nonprofit foundation dedicated to research.

Allie Kieffer is a pro runner who has had enough of body shaming. "We tell people they don't look like a runner, then discourage them from running, yet we think running would be a healthy part of their lifestyle. It's such a negative cycle," she says. Her journey focuses on emboldening others with confidence so they know a person of any body shape or size can run.

Tatyana McFadden, 17-time Paralympic medalist and 24-time major marathon winner, advocated for access to participate in track and field and speaks up for athletes with disabilities as well as adoptees.

Clare Gallagher, pro trail and ultra runner, sees running as an opportunity to champion the planet. She advocates for the environment at local political offices, and on social media and Capitol Hill. "We have to speak up on behalf of what we value, what we see, and what's worth protecting. For me, that's undeveloped land and clean air," she says.

As a runner, you have the opportunity to make a difference. Maybe on a grand scale, like some of the athletes you just read about, or maybe in small moments, like giving a high five or listening to a teammate. Maybe your biggest win will be trusting your own gut in the face of doubt.

WRITING PROMPTS

Where am I in my running journey?

What scares me, and how can I approach it with curiosity
or confidence?

My biggest hope is

My biggest challenge right now is

Who inspires me?

2

HELLO, BODY!

A RUN THROUGH THE SYSTEMS
THAT KEEP YOU MOVING

Running seems simple. One foot in front of the other, right? The reality is more complicated. When we run, bodies and minds unleash a cascade of chemical reactions and coordinated motions under force. What you need to run faster and farther is already inside of you: lungs, heart, brain, bones, muscles, tendons, cells, and self-awareness. Bonus: All of this is trainable. Parts of your ever-changing body might be stronger, less flexible, or tight. That's natural. But carefully applied stress and recovery transforms you and your moving parts!

We're going to talk about our amazing bodies: what they're made of, how they run, and how they change. Why? Because understanding your body invites you to listen to and respect it and its systems. Best of all, the more you know about your body, the better you will be able to work with—not against—your unique physiology. This is essential to staying healthy and making the most of the gifts you've been given.

In this chapter, we'll cover the systems, organs, and connections inside your body that are especially important for female runners.

NERVOUS SYSTEM: AKA BOSSY PANTS

Stand up. Run a few steps. Stop. How did that movement happen? Running starts in the brain. The brain is the boss of all your voluntary movements (such as running and giving your teammates high fives). It sits on top of your nervous system, which controls your ability to move, think, and more. The nervous system sends signals between your brain and the rest of your body through your spine and networks of nerves and cells. It is responding to stimuli it receives from both your outer and inner worlds.

One part of the nervous system is the spinal cord, which handles reflexive actions (movement that you don't have to think about) in addition to shuttling info to and from the brain. Together, neural networks called central pattern generators (CPGs) and your brain tell your muscles and joints to move.

The nervous system controls muscle activity with complex communication. Nerve cells send electrical pulses between your brain and muscles. Prewired patterns of movement—your natural running form, for example—just happen. As your brain controls the action of running, it considers sensory information—what you see, hear, and feel, along with muscle and joint feedback. That's how it decides to adjust, say, to dodge a dog on the sidewalk. (Or you choose to stop and pet it.)

When you are startled, the nervous system reacts, increasing your heart rate and releasing sugar into your blood. Stressors—school, racing, social-media notifications—may kick such responses into overdrive.

But don't let the name fool you. The nervous system also handles many of the chiller parts of life, including recovery, digestion, and healing with the parasympathetic system. To tap into this, try relaxing activities such as petting that dog, breathing deeply, journaling, and doodling.

ENDOCRINE SYSTEM: GLAND CENTRAL STATION

One of the nervous system's besties is the endocrine system, a complex network of glands, hormones, and more. It controls lots of what's happening under your skin. In fact, this system oversees your period, metabolism, development, and how you adapt to exercise—including whether you might get hurt from running. Its main goal? Tell your cells what to do. Oh, and maintain some balance!

How, exactly? Basically, the brain talks with and listens to hormones (chemical actors that send messages and play specific roles as they circulate in blood, tissues, and organs) and glands (such as the thyroid and pituitary). As hormones ebb and flow throughout the day or over weeks, they create cycles, including periods. Each of us has our own internal biological clock that produces circadian rhythms, including our sleep cycle.

CLOSER LOOK

Heya, hypothalamus

A gatekeeper in the brain is the hypothalamus, which monitors and regulates signals within the endocrine system. It keeps tabs on hormones and gland secretions that affect a wide range of functions, always aiming to preserve homeostasis (balance). When it detects changes in training, nutrition, and recovery, it adjusts levels of hormones to turn certain functions on and off. For example, your period. If you're too low on fuel, the brain lowers gonadotropin-releasing hormone (GnRH), disrupting the cascade of hormones to and from the pituitary and ovaries, stopping ovulation. (See Your Cycle, p. 23.)

MUSCULOSKELETAL SYSTEM:
PULLEYS, LEVERS, AND MOVING PARTS

Flex your arm. Feel your bicep bulging? That's a muscle, tissue that creates force and movement. Muscles are made up of fibers, and the better those fibers work with your nervous system, the more impressive your coordination, speed, and agility.

The fibers that make up your muscles are not all created equal—some excel at endurance (slow-twitch, called type I) and others at power (fast-twitch, called type II). There's not much difference between the muscle makeup of males and females when it comes to the balance of endurance- and power-oriented fibers; however, in females, the largest fibers tend to be type I. Generally, much of our lean muscle mass resides in the lower body; there's power in our hips and legs.

Flex your arm again. Feel your wrist, your hand, your fingers—a handful of the upward of 206 bones in your skeleton.

Your skeleton gives your body structure and houses two very important things: bone marrow, which makes blood cells, and minerals. Blood cells transport oxygen, the most essential fuel for your body. Bones also house calcium, a mineral needed to strengthen your skeleton; it also circulates in blood and helps with contracting your muscles.

When your muscles contract, they tug on your bones. Bones bend and flex under forces like gravity. Your bones are in flux, constantly building up and breaking down thanks in part to two types of cells (osteoblasts and osteoclasts) in concert with hormones, growth, and nutrition. One of the hormones important for bone health is estrogen. Among other roles, it supports bone cell formation and reduces breakdown.

Bone health requires a balance between these two cell types, especially when you start running and get your period. Almost all of your peak bone mass is gained in adolescence. Girls' bones build up close to their peak

Make no bones about it

Osteoporosis is a disease of weak and brittle bones that break easily. Unfortunately, being a female puts you at higher risk. Other factors include low hormone levels, menstrual dysfunction, low energy availability, small body-frame size, and smoking. Given the risk, some women elect to get annual measurements of their bone mineral density in order to keep an eye on bone health as they get older. If you've had multiple stress fractures or are concerned about your bone health, talk to a doctor.

density by age 18 and reach peak mass in the late twenties, depending on genetics and other factors. After that, bones can't create new material or strength, only maintain what's been constructed. This is why it's especially important to do what you can to increase bone density, starting now.

When your body is sufficiently fueled, and has sufficiently functioning hormones, bones respond to the stress of exercise by increasing strength and density. Running and strength training are great ways to boost bones.

Straighten and bend your leg. See how your knee connects your thigh and shin? Bones are linked by joints, like your knee—an intersection of bones with ligaments (tough tissue with nerves) and cartilage (which covers the ends of bones). Joints cushion, roll, glide, and provide valuable feedback to the brain.

Point and flex your foot. Feel the sinewy section above your heel and below your calf that shortens and extends? That's your Achilles tendon. Bones are linked to muscles by tendons, connective tissue that stores and releases energy like a spring. Other connective tissue, called fascia, also interacts with muscles and nerves. Feel that on the bottom of your foot, where runners could always use a massage!

CARDIOVASCULAR SYSTEM: THE HUB

Take a deep breath, in, then out. Each time you inhale, your lungs extract oxygen from the breath. Your lungs then work with your heart and an intricate network to deliver that oxygen to the rest of your body. Blood moves through blood vessels, itty-bitty pipelike tubes including arteries, veins, and capillaries. If you lined up an average-sized kid's blood vessels, they'd make a 60,000-mile line, and an adult's would stretch nearly 100,000 miles.

Your heart is your body's pump. First, using electrical signals, it pumps blood into your lungs to pick up oxygen. Second, it pumps blood through your body and back to your lungs with gas waste to be breathed out. Each time you exhale, your body expels carbon dioxide, which is produced by your hardworking cells.

Heart rate is the frequency of your heartbeats—the number of times it pumps in one minute. Your heartbeat when you are at rest might be somewhere between 40 and 100 beats per minute. While that number

What should my heart rate be when I'm running?

It depends, but it's likely not the same as your teammate's. First, heart rate is an incredibly variable number, influenced by age, size, genetics, fitness, dehydration, and more. Second, figuring out your heart-rate zones for running—say, at hard, medium, and easy paces—takes testing and experimentation. A simple equation (220 minus your age) will produce a very big ballpark guesstimate of max heart rate, but if you'll be using heart rate in training, your coach should help you find your max heart rate with a careful test (perhaps running hills hard, a time trial, or a visit to a physiology lab). The most important factor? Listening to your body by paying attention to your breathing rate and other indicators of how hard you're working.

Turn on your heart light

When Melody runs, she focuses her attention on the back of her heart. She says that focusing there lends a lightness to her step.

I go deeper and run from inside my heart. I am the blood traveling to and from hardworking organs. This mindfulness exercise helps me stay present and focused. Focus on your heart and you will notice its beat in sync with the heartbeat of the earth. —M.F.

---

can be altered by caffeine, illness, and other factors, it is a helpful guide. When running moderately or hard, the tissues in your body need more oxygen and fuel, and your heart rate increases. So does the amount of blood your heart pumps per beat.

Based on medical research, women's hearts and lungs tend to be smaller than men's. Basically, this means our engines are smaller. We have lower diastolic pressure (part of the force at which the heart pumps oxygen-rich blood to the body) and lower maximum heart rates. We breathe more, which requires more work when compared to our male running buddies and correlates to lower VO_2 max, one metric of fitness (see Chapter 4).

DIGESTIVE SYSTEM: THE INS AND OUTS

What goes in must come out—that is, if it's not used or stored by your digestive system, aka the gastrointestinal (GI) system. When you eat and drink food, this nutrition-gleaning system breaks the solids and liquids down so that it can transport what's needed around your body, absorb and store fuel, and expel the rest. From your mouth and stomach to gallbladder and intestine, many a moving part helps break down carbs, protein, fat, vitamins, minerals, and liquids into essential energy. One important player found in your digestive tract is bacteria, which breaks down food but also works closely with your brain and endocrine and immune systems.

ENERGY SYSTEMS: CHARGE!

When your phone is low on battery, it needs a charge. When you're hungry, you need a snack. When you're running, your body needs a power source. Living and moving require energy! Our tiny cells and big muscles all need fuel, even for the smallest movements. To contract, muscles need essential fuel called ATP (which is short for adenosine triphosphate). We have a limited storage of it. That's where your body's energy systems come in. Our body recycles and reuses products, sort of like a power or recycling plant, to continually re-create ATP.

Your body has several such power plants, energy systems that use and circulate fuel in different ways, but work together. Your immediate energy systems include several power plants that rely on chemical reactions, without oxygen, and supply only 5 to 15 seconds of contractions (think: a short sprint). It takes them much longer than that to recover and replenish their supply.

Another system, your anaerobic system, also runs without oxygen— like when your effort is hard enough to make you want to stop. It produces energy quickly, but requires sugar for its own fuel. To produce energy, this system runs through complex chemical reactions with glucose (carbohydrate, aka sugar, in your blood) or glycogen (sugar stored in your muscles and liver) to make ATP. As a power plant, the anaerobic system provides intermediate speed and delivers enough energy for intense work for short bouts. It can fuel up to two minutes of hard work but leaves by-products around.

CLOSER LOOK

Working on your fitness

Did you know that running events longer than two minutes are primarily aerobic? That's why building your aerobic capacity with easy and steady running is essential—not only when beginning a training program but also throughout your running journey.

Your aerobic system runs on oxygen, but it needs sugar (in the form of glucose or glycogen) to power your runs. It requires lots of steps (and more time than the anaerobic system) but is a clean power plant without many by-products. And it's prolific, making a lot of ATP when compared to the other power plants. The aerobic system can also use fat and protein as another fuel. For the record, fat is hard to break down, your body can only use it at low to moderate intensities, and protein must be stolen from elsewhere (like muscles, yikes!) to be converted to energy.

BIOMECHANICS: LOCOMOTION POTION

How, exactly, do you move through space? With a cascade of chemical reactions that propels your body forward. While running may feel automatic, your body actually is dealing with invisible forces and other factors when you run. Your movement requires coordination, controlling specific motions and masses under forces like gravity. Whether your stride is bouncy or elongated, whether your arms swing low or knees knock in, your nervous system is constantly seeking the easiest path and orchestrating your stride.

Forces affect movement. When we run, forces that are as much as three times our weight act on one leg at a time. We also face lateral (side to side), acceleration (speeding up), and deceleration (slowing down) forces. That's when the structures of our bones and joints and movements of our muscles and tendons are called to act. Their goal? To counter and stabilize the forces and to keep propelling us where we choose to go or wherever the course flags point us!

If some joints or muscles lack control or aren't firing, they can become sloppy, wasting energy and potentially causing wear and tear. That's why experts encourage runners to work on things like stability, mobility, and strength to improve form and efficiency (see Chapter 3).

REPRODUCTIVE SYSTEM: PUBERTY, PERIODS, AND BEYOND

Say it with us. Pube. Er. Tee. Puberty! It's a natural process. It's a rite of passage. It's part of becoming a stronger athlete and human. And yet people don't seem to want to talk about it. Or when they do talk about it, it feels awkward.

I feared puberty. I was a runner applauded for being "thin," so a changing body, including getting my period, was like an approaching dark, ominous storm that terrified me. I spent a lot of energy thinking about how to avoid it. If someone had explained to me that I could embrace it rather than resist it, I believe my self-confidence would have been much greater.

Honor yourself, including the bodily functions that just so happen to be responsible for the continuation of the human race! As women, our cycles teach us how to literally go with the flow. Every cycle we experience—periods and beyond—prepares us to be adaptable and able to respond to an ever-changing world. They give us full capacity for living and loving in our lives. —M.F.

Puberty is the phase of life when a child's body matures and gains the ability to reproduce. When puberty arrives—usually somewhere between age 8 and 13 for girls and generally later for boys—it sparks development with a surge of human growth hormone (HGH). HGH teams up with other hormones to trigger development of your breasts and reproductive system. Girls gain height and weight as they build bone, muscle, and fat. Puberty brings mental, social, and emotional changes too.

The process of growing into adulthood (called adolescence) includes puberty and lasts until your midtwenties. Weathering so many changes may feel overwhelming, especially at first, but you're not alone. Your teammates might be experiencing and figuring out puberty themselves. Adults might be adjusting to the idea of you growing up.

Take it from women who've gone before: You can thrive during and after puberty. With tools, resources, and a little practice, you'll gain newfound power. In some cultures around the world, puberty and the arrival of a first period is something that families and communities celebrate!

During puberty, your body changes. A lot. The reality is, though, that we are constantly changing! As babies, as teens, as adults, our bodies are in a state of flux. Sometimes it's just more obvious.

Your body type—short, tall, big-boned, or small-framed—is a result of lots of things, including genetics (what your parents and ancestors passed along to you), the activities you do, how you fuel, and even socioeconomics. Every body is different, and it's very hard to tell whether someone is "healthy" by looking at them. But there are some similarities among women. Generally, women have more body fat than men, thanks to childbearing features. Fat gets a bad rap, but the truth is body fat isn't something to be shunned. In fact, it serves multiple important purposes. Fat generates hormones and is also found in nerves, bone marrow, and organs. It's essential!

PRO TIP

Your body is constantly speaking to you; your job is to learn to listen.

For girls, puberty often starts with development of breast buds—small, firm lumps under the nipples—which might feel tender or even hurt. One bud might grow faster than the other; both might not grow at the same rate as your friends'. And that's absolutely OK.

Puberty may also be signaled by the growth of pubic and underarm hair, as well as a changing body shape. You might notice a new thickness around your middle section. Your body is adding weight and will typically redistribute it elsewhere, like in breasts and hips, during this multi-year process.

Increased hormones trigger the menstrual cycle—*voilà*! Your period starts a year or two (or three) after puberty begins. Two of the main hormones involved in the menstrual cycle, estrogen and progesterone, play big roles in your overall development, including building bone strength, cardiovascular health, and mood regulation. As these and other hormones fluctuate, they may influence your mood, appetite, and other processes in your body. Hormone fluctuations might also contribute to fatigue or pain, such as cramps, bloating, and headaches, before or during your period.

Emerging research suggests hormones may influence your athletic performance throughought the menstrual cycle. Hormones affect physiological functions including metabolism, heat regulation, and joint performance. So you may notice changes in your training, racing, fueling, recovery, and your risk of getting sick or hurt. (See Chapter 5 for an in-depth rundown on what to expect when running throughout your

GO WITH THE FLOW

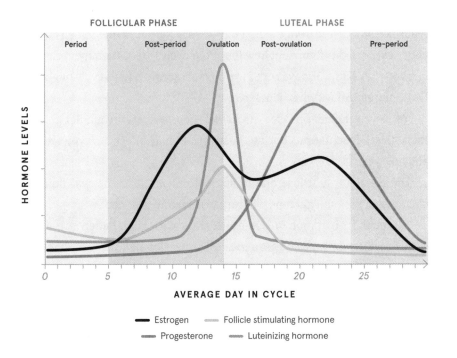

FOLLICULAR PHASE | **LUTEAL PHASE**

Period | Post-period | Ovulation | Post-ovulation | Pre-period

HORMONE LEVELS

AVERAGE DAY IN CYCLE

0   5   10   15   20   25

— Estrogen   — Follicle stimulating hormone
— Progesterone   — Luteinizing hormone

cycle.) There's still a lot to learn about our cycles and how they affect us and our running, since sports science and medical research has often excluded female athletes. But you've got an essential indicator of health and performance: your own body and mind.

YOUR CYCLE

When your period first comes, it might be hard to predict. You might have irregular signs and symptoms, such as a late or early period or changes in the amount and duration of bleeding. Track your period and symptoms—

which are signals of health and growth—in a training log or app to note what's happening for you and learn about your body's own patterns.

The cycle, on average, goes like this: Day 1 is the first day of bleeding (your period). Count from the first day of your period to the first day of your next period to figure out how long your cycles are. Generally, cycles last between 21 and 35 days with 2 to 8 days of bleeding. But a cycle might be as long as 45 days when it first starts.

Your cycle includes phases—follicular (first), ovulation (middle), and luteal (last). Fluctuations during those phases may affect how you feel and how you run.

On average, you'll lose one to six tablespoons of menstrual fluid during each period. That fluid will vary in color and texture.

Although it's common for some girls to have irregular patterns from cycle to cycle, take note and see a medical professional if you experience any of the following:

> Your periods are very heavy and you have to change tampons or pads every hour
> Your periods are frequently unpredictable or abnormal or disrupt your ability to go about daily life
> You're feeling light-headed or dizzy
> You haven't gotten a period by age 16
> Your cycle is less than 21 days or more than 45 days
> You experience severe pain, anxiety, or depression before or during your period
> You bleed between periods
> Your periods have stopped

Red flags

Amenorrhea is the medical term for missing menstrual cycles. Although it may be common among runners, it's a red flag—not a badge of honor. Missing periods are often a call to seek professional help. This issue presents in a few ways. Here are diagnoses you might hear from a doctor:

* If you've yet to get a period by age 16, that's called *primary amenorrhea*.
* If you've started your period and then miss it for at least six months, that's called *secondary amenorrhea*.
* If you get fewer than nine periods per year, that's called *oligomenorrhea*.

If you skip or miss a period, heads up! It might not mean anything, especially if you are in the first year or two of having a period. It might mean you're pregnant. (If you're sexually active, your first line of action is taking a pregnancy test.) Or it might be related to taking birth control pills or other medication, illness, stress, exercising a lot, or not eating enough. When your body is stressed, such as if it is underfueled and training hard, it does its best to survive and conserves whatever energy it can to preserve key functions (like your heart beating and your brain thinking). That's why it may shut off several functions and disrupt specific hormone messengers, including those that trigger your period.

Lacking a cycle or missing periods (called *amenorrhea*) is a key sign that the balance of your hormones has been thrown off and your body is under stress. You should seek medical insight if your periods are MIA or fit the signs on p. 24.

Dang, our bodies are legit marvels! They deserve our respect. Understanding and listening to a constantly changing body is an essential skill for any athlete. It's a practice that can help you run smarter, stronger, and faster. Ultimately, this practice fosters acceptance as you grow into the healthy, thriving human you are.

WRITING PROMPTS

When I run, I feel

My favorite body part is

What I've heard about puberty and what I now know

My first period

Today I will appreciate, respect, and honor my body in these ways

3

TRAIN LIKE A BOSS

THE MAGIC OF WORK AND REST

The first thing to know about training? There's no secret formula or perfect way to do it. Furthermore, what works for one person might not work for you. So that means you've got options! Or as your grandma might say, there's more than one way to skin a cat. (Don't take her literally; cats are too cute to skin.)

As both coaches and athletes, we've witnessed and experimented with a wide range of training approaches. Emerging research, including a focus on female athletes, reveals more insights than ever about exercise science. What we present in this and the following chapter is based on research blended with our combined years of experience.

When it comes to training, this much is crystal clear: Progress results from a combination of work and rest. These two factors are essential if you want to grow, improve, and adapt as an athlete (and as a human too).

No matter what, the most important training method is your own one-person, ongoing study of you. Like science, training requires trial and error. It's testing a hypothesis (in a messy lab with countless distracting factors) and being curious about results. In this experiment, tuning in to your body and mind is key.

In this chapter, we'll share our approach to work and rest, including the nuts and bolts of how to train and recover. You'll learn about effort, form, mileage, strength work and crosstraining, drills, rest days, active recovery, sleep, and more—all of which lead to the adaptations we'll talk about in the next chapter. Let's dive in.

WORK: RUNNING

Running is work, a special kind of work. It's the kind that tests your mettle, pushes your limits, increases your ability to use oxygen, boosts your strength, and builds your fitness—all perks that help runners progress.

Effective training requires a range of work, which is essentially a variety of stress. This includes any activity that requires a specific effort (think: long runs, track workouts, strength training, even easy jogs). Each effort should target a particular fitness goal, such as endurance, strength, or speed. It might feel hard, uncomfortable, or tedious. It might make you feel tired, sore, or a little pukey.

Sometimes going hard is the point of a workout, but not always. In fact, that should be a fraction of the time you spend training. Melody's rule of thumb: *Train, don't strain.* Going superduper, seeing-stars hard should be reserved for extra-special times, like certain race days.

Be tough, absolutely, but not to the point that you hurt yourself. For example, there's no need to run through sharp, stabbing, or otherwise acute injury pain, especially the type that alters your stride—that's the type of pain that'll sideline you (see Q: Is it OK to run through pain? p. 64).

Running work varies by frequency (how often), intensity (how hard), and duration (how long). It loads your body with micro-traumas. It taxes your engine (the cardiovascular system, which delivers oxygen and

Measure your work with effort levels

Training requires working different systems. One way to measure the work you're doing is to use a rate of perceived exertion, first coined in a numeric scale by scientist Gunnar Borg. Perceived exertion—aka effort—is the most dependable indicator runners can use and frees you up from fixating on paces and splits. Sure, hundredths of a second have their place, but hand-timing, wonky GPS, and such are not always reliable. Practice measuring your own perceived exertion while training.

Here's a sample spectrum of perceived running efforts to consider:

* Very easy—could do it all day
* Easy—chatty, conversational effort
* Steady—comfortably uncomfortable, still talking in sentences
* Moderate—focused, strong, talking a few words at a time
* Hard—tough, hard to talk
* Fast—approaching top speed, can't talk (but maybe can yell "Track!" so people clear out of lane one)

nutrients throughout your body) and your carriage (like a chassis, or body of a car, including your muscles). Workouts are designed to create a faster, more powerful engine and a stronger, more resilient carriage, when paired with recovery.

Once your body has adapted to running (this takes at least a few months) the majority of your running work should be at an easy effort. Why? Because that's how you target the specific adaptations that'll help you improve as a middle- and long-distance runner. Depending on where you are in your career and season, a mix of running and nonrunning work and a range of effort levels should vary to meet specific goals. We'll talk more about the big picture (periodization) and specific types of running workouts in the next chapter, but for now, just know that when it comes to running, you've got more gears than a bike.

RUNNING FORM

When you run, you have a natural stride. The brain and body do their best to run as efficiently as possible, whether a runner high-steps, arm-flails, or does something else that looks a bit wonky. Lots of factors, including posture, balance, mobility, strength, fatigue, and history of injury influence your form.

To get a feel for your own form, try running barefoot, working up to strides (short bouts of faster running; see p. 59), either on a track or grass infield. Pay attention to details you might not normally notice: Does your foot slap the ground? What's up with your toes? Is your core engaged?

Once you've got a sense of what you're doing naturally, play a little! Explore feeling your top, medium, and slow speeds, and your liftoff and stride length, powered by the springs in your feet, ankles, legs, and hips. Ask a teammate to video you so you can see and assess your form, and maybe even get feedback from a coach or physical therapist.

Maybe you've been told that to run better, you should land a certain way. Don't worry about where, exactly, your foot hits the ground, such as on the heel or forefoot. Research has shown that thinking about changing how you land is distracting and might even cause injuries. There are other ways to make your steps smoother and more efficient. When you run, the big drivers of movement are your hips and core. So increasing strength and range of motion in these areas can improve your posture and stride (see Work: Beyond Running, p. 40).

Here are form cues to try when you're out on a run. No need to think about everything at once; rather, focus on one cue at a time:

> Light, quick, quiet steps
> Run tall (imagine someone pulling you toward the sky by a single hair on top of your head)
> Keep eyes on the horizon, shoulders down
> Swing your arms back
> Let your feet fall under your hips (you're not kicking a soccer ball!)
> Relax (can you feel your cheeks wiggle?)

MILEAGE

How many miles should you run? It depends. What works for a team-mate or competitor might not work for your body. Melody ran 25 to 45 miles per week in high school, emphasizing quality over quantity and found it worked well for her, allowing her to perform at her best and avoid injury. Pro Sara Hall, on the other hand, ran 70 miles per week

---

Mix it up

PRO TIP

Where you run depends a lot on where you live or go to school. But whenever possible, vary the type of terrain you cover. Running on different surfaces and slopes improves your form by strengthening your feet and challenging your proprioception, your body's ability to sense its position and movement. When you can, seek out green spaces—research has shown that trees can make you happier! If you are limited in where you can run but have access to a treadmill, be sure to vary the grade (slope) to better approximate running outside and avoid overusing the same muscles.

during high school. Every athlete is different. Some are more durable; others more susceptible to injuries, especially when ramping up volume. If you're increasing mileage, pay attention to your energy levels and other markers of recovery and performance to find your sweet spot—knowing that your limits might change over time (see Q: How can I tell if I'm recovering enough? p. 39).

REST

Rest means recovery, and FYI, rest is not laziness. It is the time when your body adapts to training—when you reap the rewards of work, like a farmer harvesting a crop. Without adequate recovery—including easy days, sleep, and total rest—training adaptations go down the tubes. Your muscles, nerves, bones, fascia, and mind need this time to repair before they can progress, strengthen, or improve. Certain activities, like swimming, jogging, and yin yoga, can aid in your recovery by promoting circulation and relaxation. Mobility and stretching are other so-called active recovery methods, which we'll cover in a minute. The best example of rest is the kind where you truly rest, doing little to no exercise. If the word *rest* rubs you the wrong way, think of it as *recharge* time. No matter what you call it, it is essential to realizing your potential.

Depending on your age, how long you've been running, and where you are in a training cycle, you might need more or less rest. As you get stronger or fitter, you might notice that you recover faster. Woo-hoo!

PRO TIP

Take 48 to 72 hours of recovery between hard workouts.

That means you'll feel less sore and tired between runs and stronger heading into your key workouts.

RUNNING DOWNTIME

What do you do when you're not running? Maybe eat, sleep, read, go to school, TikTok, hang with the fam, work? Regardless, everything you do adds up. Imagine your time and energy like a pie. Each activity takes up a slice. You have only one pie. And it's on you to slice it up, whether it's pumpkin or cherry. The reality? No one can "do it all," and your body doesn't distinguish between stressors like school activities, family drama, and running hard. Stress is stress. Knowing that, what is your biggest slice?

Remember: To make the most of running, especially with the 27,593 other things you have going on, you need to protect a slice for rest and recovery. When you're resting, know you don't have to be busy recovering—say, ice bathing, foam-rolling, or scouring best-in-state times. Give yourself a break! Consider giving your social media scrolling a break too. Quieting your mind and body is as important as pushing and moving them. In stillness, you are able to fill the reservoirs of energy you need to perform. Research suggests that silent downtime can help restore your brain, nerves, energy, heart, and lungs. When we get quiet and are free from distractions, we are able to better hear our own powerful voice within: intuition (see Intuition: Trust Your Gut, p. 174).

SLEEP SWEET SLEEP

Sleep is where the magic happens. There are many tools and gadgets that are promoted as recovery tools, but the best use of your downtime? Good, solid shut-eye.

Sleep is recovery for life and training. Without sufficient sleep, well-being is compromised. Lack of sleep can affect performance, academics, judgment, and even bone health. It may also affect whether you get hurt or sick.

Do you feel tired or sleepy during the day? Studies show that most teenagers fall short on sleep. Experts suggest *at least* 9 to 10 hours of sleep for optimal development and recovery. You'll know you're getting enough when you wake up feeling rested and when you can stay alert during the day. Research suggests that athletes who get quality sleep have better reaction times, decision-making, and endurance. Sleep also allows your growth hormones to get to work, improving both mental and physical development, recovery and adaptations from training, and even your mood. You'll feel better—and do better in school, running, and relationships—if you get a good night's sleep.

You might have trouble falling asleep, especially after hard or long efforts. Or you might be stuck with a routine that doesn't fit with your natural sleep tendencies (especially if you're a night owl forced to wake up at the crack of dawn for school). That's tough, but there are ways to get more—even if it means taking a quick siesta or giving up a show or social media time. If you're suffering from insomnia or chronically tired, get checked out by a doc.

To improve the quality of your z's, try the following suggestions.

Create a sleep cave. The best environment for sleeping is a cool, dark, quiet space. Get an alarm clock so you can keep your phone elsewhere; it's distracting and disruptive to a good night's sleep.

Design a bedtime routine. Try to stick to a regular schedule with bed- and wake-up times. Create sleep-inducing habits: An hour or two before bed, turn off screens. Limit blue light, which disrupts your body's sleep mechanisms, or set a filter on your phone or computer if you must be on it late. Wind down with relaxing activities, like foam-rolling, journaling, doodling, listening to chill music, or taking a warm bath. Have a snack or soothing warm drink with protein (think: warm milk) to promote muscle recovery.

Pass on supplements. If you consume caffeine, stop by noon (see Coffee break, p. 139). Also, know that over-the-counter supplements and prescription medications can interfere with your sleep cycle, so be aware of potential side effects. The jury's out on how sleep aids affect performance. Even some teas could give you wacky dreams, so err on the side of caution.

Nap if you can. Even a short snooze can improve your energy and mood. Aim to keep naps to no more than 30 minutes, earlier in the day, to avoid staring at the ceiling at night.

Give yourself a break. Find little ways to take a break where you can. Even if you're working hard on a paper or rushing from track to choir, can

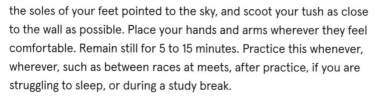

Legs up the wall

PRO TIP

This restorative yoga pose is relaxing and rejuvenating. Sit next to a wall, either on a bed or on the floor. Swing your legs up the wall with the soles of your feet pointed to the sky, and scoot your tush as close to the wall as possible. Place your hands and arms wherever they feel comfortable. Remain still for 5 to 15 minutes. Practice this whenever, wherever, such as between races at meets, after practice, if you are struggling to sleep, or during a study break.

you lie down for a minute? Just putting your legs up the wall for five minutes can be restorative. Consider whether that essay will be more coherent if you wake up early instead of burning the midnight oil.

REST DAYS: CHILL OUT!

Rest days are the best days. There are two types: rest days that include some light activity, such as a very easy jog or swim or stretching; and rest days that are totally off—in other words, no crosstraining, no nothing. With all the growing you are doing as a young athlete, we highly recommend the latter at least once per week. As Melody recommends, *No stress, just rest*. Doing nothing may be a weird feeling at first, but we promise you'll get the hang of it and probably come to really enjoy it.

How many rest days you need changes over time. For example, in middle school, a healthy plan might be to run two to four days a week, play other sports on other days, and keep at least one total rest day. In high school, you might run up to five days a week, with one day a week for crosstraining and one total rest day.

PRO TIP

Resting heart rate

Some people use resting heart rate (RHR) as a signal that it's time for extra rest. You can find your RHR by counting your pulse first thing in the morning. Before you sit up, find your pulse in your neck; count the number of pulses for 15 seconds and multiply by four (or count for 60 seconds) to find your RHR. After a few weeks you will get an idea of what's average for you. If your RHR increases, it might indicate you're not recovered, are fighting an illness, or are dealing with stress. Tread lightly.

No matter your age, taking a totally restorative day per week, with no exercise or workouts, can encourage both physical and mental recovery. Especially as you are growing, your body—muscles, nerves, bones, and brain—needs time to recover from all that you've done in training (and everything else you're busy with). How much time you need to recover depends on a bunch of factors, including sleep, nutrition, how long you've been running, and stress levels. Listen to your body's signals.

How can I tell if I'm recovering enough?

Running and training hard will make you feel sore and tired. But you shouldn't feel sore or tired all the time. If you feel persistently sore in the same spot or tired and fatigued consistently for more than two days, it's a sign from your body that it's overstressed. You might need more fuel, more rest, or to do less training. You might be in a tough phase of your hormonal cycle. You also might have increased life stress (think: finals or a breakup).

If you notice sudden, persistent, or severe changes in the following factors, speak up:

* Resting heart rate (see Pro Tip: Resting heart rate, p. 38)
* Mood
* Energy level
* Cravings
* Soreness or pain

* Weight or shape
* Sleep
* Motivation or enthusiasm
* Overall well-being (for example, head rushes or light-headedness are red flags)

Jot these specifics in your training log, and pay attention to patterns that emerge, especially around your period. If you suspect you're not recovering enough, keep your coach in the loop, so she or he can adjust your training if needed. Work with a trusted resource (see Chapter 10 for a list of ideas) to see what puzzle pieces may need to be rearranged.

Think about rest days as an investment in the work you've done and what's to come. Take an extra day if you need it. Trust us, you'll emerge restored and refreshed.

WORK: BEYOND RUNNING

The best way to get better at running is to run. But certain nonrunning activities can be really helpful. They can increase your strength and resilience and improve your runs. Here we will look at activities to squeeze around your runs, such as dynamic moves, drills, strength training, and crosstraining. As with your running work, nonrunning training stress also varies by frequency, intensity, and duration.

DYNAMIC MOVES

These activities are like multitools, super useful in many ways. The following examples are our go-tos for engaging muscles and mind simultaneously, increasing coordination, and boosting mobility and stability. Whether you do them as part of a warm-up routine or after runs, a little dynamic diligence can go a long way.

Activation exercises. These exercises turn your muscles on and engage your mind. After long bouts of inactivity, such as during sleep or a drive or sitting in class, activation exercises will wake everything up before you hit the ground running. Exercises such as planks, clamshells, and hip bridges are ideal because they activate the core, hips, and glutes (the gluteal muscles of your booty)—all especially important for runners. Practice good form (quality over quantity!), and add resistance (with rubber resistance bands) as you progress. You can do these most days of the week.

Dynamic stretches. These not only get you warmed up, but also improve mobility and coordination. Examples include knee to chest, heel to butt, over/under hurdles, leg swings, and bear crawl. Your coach might sprinkle these into your warm-up routine. You can do these most days too.

Drills and skips. These faster movements promote improved running efficiency and form. They train your neuromuscular system, strengthen your hips and other muscles, and promote range of motion. Our favorite drills include high knees, butt kickers, grapevine (aka carioca), and A, B, and C skips. Your team might do these as part of a warm-up during practice. Incorporate drills and skips up to three times a week, before or after a run or workout.

Plyometrics. Plyos are fast, explosive movements such as jumps, hops, and skips. Plyos increase power and bone, tendon, and ligament strength. Good form and speed are imperative. A few favorites are bounding, one-legged jumps, box jumps, and burpees. Because mechanics are important, you should do these with the supervision of a coach, and prioritize strength training over these if you're pressed for time. Once you've nailed the technique, incorporate these once or more a week, depending on where you are in your season.

WARMING UP

The first few minutes of a run don't have to suck. In fact, they shouldn't! That's why we warm up with routines designed to get our bodies and our brains ready to run. A proper warm-up increases your blood flow and heart rate, which helps deliver oxygen and nutrients to the systems that are about to be put to work. A thorough routine also wakes up your central nervous system, your muscles and other soft tissues, and even your organs.

Dynamic warm-up movements can help improve your performance and may prevent injuries. Most importantly, warm-up routines make you feel good—physically and mentally—and can bring peace of mind and calm nerves.

There are a bajillion combinations of activities you can do to warm up. Whatever routine you use should be tailored to the workout you're about to do, whether it's an easy run, a speed workout, a race, strength work, or crosstraining. Include low-key movement like easy running or walking along with dynamic stretches and muscle activation. You can also add in mobility work, drills, or strides. If you have specific physical therapy exercises, add them to your warm-up as well, unless instructed otherwise by your physical therapist.

Your team might have a group warm-up; participate! On meet days, before your event, you may need to warm up again. Experiment with the distance, duration, and range of movements that work best for you. You know you're ready when you're sweating, your core is engaged, and you're getting into a rhythm.

If you're crunched for time, even just 60 seconds of movement can help wake up your body. In a pinch, try a minute of foam-rolling, core activation, a few push-ups, sun salutations, or even dancing.

Melody's Warm-Up Routine

This routine includes activation exercises for your core, glutes, and hips, plus drills and strides. You don't need any equipment but you can use light to heavy resistance bands during the activation exercises as you gain strength. Before easy runs, do the dynamic moves listed below (up to skipping), then hit the road. Before tougher workouts and races, add 5 to 15 minutes of easy running after the activation, then do the skips and drills, plus 4 or more strides (see p. 59) with full recovery.

Plank × 2. Get in a push-up position, with your belly drawn into your spine and buttocks squeezed to support your lower back. Draw your shoulder blades down and together, away from your ears. Look at the floor and lengthen through the back of your neck. Breathe normally as you hold for 15–30 sec. Rest 30 sec.; repeat.

Clamshells × 3. Lie on your side, with your knees bent and aligned, hips and shoulders stacked, feet together. Keep your heels touching as you slowly lift your top knee by rotating your thigh from the hip. Go as high as you can without tilting your torso and hip backward. Feel your jeans' butt-pocket muscle activate. Hold this position at the top, working up to 60 sec. Slowly return your knee to where it started. Repeat 2 more times and switch sides. When this is easy, add resistance with a band.

Hip Bridge × 3. Lie on your back, with your knees bent and hip-width apart, feet planted on the ground a foot length from your buttocks, with your arms extended down to 45 degrees from each side. Breathe in. As you exhale, press your feet into the floor, rolling your spine off the ground, until your body weight is supported by your feet and shoulders. Squeeze your booty and hold for 10 sec. Release with control to the floor. Repeat twice more. When this feels easy, extend one leg straight out while in the bridge, and hold for 5 sec., each side.

Fire Hydrant × 3. Begin on your hands and knees in a tabletop position, with your knees hip-width apart, belly activated to spine, and back of your neck lengthened. Keep your hips level (as if a cup of tea were balanced on your lower back) as you lift one knee slightly; then rotate and lift that thigh from the hip (not your whole pelvis) until it's parallel with the ground. This will bring your knee out to the side, like a dog peeing on a fire hydrant. Hold, working up to 60 sec. Repeat twice more and switch sides. When this is easy, add a resistance band around your thighs.

Tabletop with Forward Hurdle 2 × 8. In tabletop, on your hands and knees, extend one leg straight behind you. Feel your glute engage as you hold your leg out, toes pointed downward. Turn your toes outward, bend your knee, sweep your leg forward, as if going over a hurdle next to you, and bring your knee to rest on floor. Repeat 7 more times and then switch sides.

Squat Holds × 3. If using a band, place it around both legs, above your knees. Stand with your feet a bit wider than shoulder-width. Press your hips back as if you are going to sit in a chair, and then lower them until your knees are at 90 degrees. Push your knees out to avoid letting them collapse in (against the band, if using). Feel weight in your heels, big toes, and pinky toes. Hold for 60 sec., then return to standing. When this feels easy, progress with resistance bands.

Skipping 2 × 20 yards each
(Note: Include before tougher workouts and races)

> **A Skip:** Generating power from your glutes and keeping your core engaged, skip forward while driving one knee and the opposite arm up to 90-degree angles. Think of bouncing or popping off the ground. Continue by alternating legs and arms, keeping toes flexed to the sky.

> **B Skip:** Repeat A skip, but add a pawing motion with the driving leg. That is, extend and sweep your leg to land under your hips (imagine a bull getting ready to charge).

> **C Skip:** Repeat A skip, driving one knee up and forward, but after dropping your foot to the ground, pop it back up while driving the same knee to the side, opening your hip. Alternate legs. Keep a tiny hop going on each foot the entire time, with your core engaged and upper body tall.

> **Skip with Arm Circles Forward:** Skip for height while circling both arms forward.

> **Skip with Arm Circles Backward:** Skip for height while circling both arms backward.

> **Grapevine/Carioca:** Turn 90 degrees so you're prepared to move laterally (side to side). Drive one knee up and over the opposite leg as you side-skip in one direction. Let your arms swing. Return facing the same way, leading with the alternate knee.

COOLING DOWN

After a workout or race, it's a good idea to cool down (or "warm down"). Usually consisting of 5 to 20 minutes of easy running, a cooldown helps both your body and mind wind down from the stress endured. The sooner you relax, the sooner the adaptations from your workout can take place. What's more, easy running post-workout adds to your aerobic base and is built-in time to catch up with your teammates.

STRENGTH TRAINING: POWER UP!

Strength training—aka resistance or weight training—trains your muscles, creates new connections with your nervous system, helps your bones, and regulates your hormones. (And no, it won't make you look like the Rock.)

Even better, strength training can improve your running economy and help you run faster. In some athletes, strength training has also been linked to decreased injury risk.

You can use your own body weight or heavy things like dumbbells, kettlebells, and medicine balls for resistance. You can lift hard and heavy to focus more on strength, power, and coordination, or you can string together exercises (aka circuit training) for a cardio effect.

Great strength exercises for runners include squats, deadlifts, lunges, pull-ups, and push-ups. Always focus on good form, full range of motion, and appropriate speed, depending on the exercise. Ask a strength coach to show you proper technique and mechanics.

Like running, strength work requires progression and specific cycles (periodization) to create new adaptations. Start with bodyweight exercises to nail the technique, then progress by adding weight to continue to build strength. At certain points in the year, you should focus on maintenance (not increasing stress) and also recovery—which your coach should help with. Generally, aim for two strength workouts a week. Even 5 to 15 minutes is better than nothing!

University of Massachusetts Lowell head sports performance coach Kevin Cronin encourages athletes to start a strength routine early in their careers. "It does not have to be advanced; it just needs to develop overall strength of lower and upper body along with fundamental movement patterns—squatting, lunging, pressing, pulling, and hinging," he says.

Strength training should include core work because the core is fundamental for runners. Aim for about three core sessions weekly. But we're not talking about doing crunches to get six-pack abs. You want to engage the transverse abdominal muscle (TA), your deep abs. This muscle connects and stabilizes your torso and pelvis and wraps around your front and side. To find it, fake a cough. Feel your torso flex? That's your TA. You can practice engaging the TA by lying on the ground, with your knees bent and feet on the floor, and blowing up a balloon. Or pretend that your little brother is about to punch you below your belly button; activate your lower abs to prepare for it.

Practice engaging your TA whenever, wherever, until you don't have to think about it. The aim? Create a stronger, more stable core so your glutes, hip flexors, and other body parts can move well.

Try this simple but powerful 5-minute routine: Aim for 3+ core sessions each week.

Dead Bug 2 × 10 each side. Lie on your back. Engage your TA, pulling your belly button toward your spine. Lift your knees, and bend them to 90 degrees with your feet in the air; extend your right arm and left leg away from each other while lifting your head off the floor to engage your upper abs without arching your back. Breathe. Alternate sides. Repeat.

Spiderman 2 × 5 each side. From a high plank position, first do 3 push-ups (from knees if needed). Then, from the plank position, bring your right knee to the outside of your right elbow, then extend your leg straight back and hold it in the air for 3 sec. Switch sides. Repeat.

Plank Rotation 2 × 5 each side. From a high plank position, rotate onto one hand and the outside edge of your stacked feet. (To make it easier, you can put one foot in front of the other or rest the bottom knee on the ground under your hip.) Extend your arm to the sky. Hold for 10 sec., pushing your obliques (the muscles on the sides of your torso) upward. Keep your hips and core engaged, with your spine and body in a straight line from head to hips to ankles. For an added challenge, lift your top leg from the side plank. Switch sides.

CROSSTRAINING: MIX IT UP!

Crosstraining isn't only for injured runners. While it's an option for staying fit when you can't run, it is also useful for runners who are not ready to run every day or who aren't otherwise increasing mileage. Furthermore, certain nonrunning activities can help you improve as a runner. No- or low-impact exercise, such as biking, swimming, and yoga, can increase fitness without the high-impact pounding of running. It can also help aid recovery and strengthen muscle groups that are complementary to running. Remember to honor rest and recovery; something is not always better than nothing!

Here are a few crosstraining options, along with sample workouts.

Pool running

Use a flotation belt so that you can focus on high cadence (leg turnover) and form. Extend each leg fully with every stride-like movement, envisioning the pawing motion of touching the ground and quickly pulling it through. Counting your "steps" can help you gauge your effort. (FYI, it won't look like running on land, but you shouldn't look like a jellyfish, either.) Engaging your TA is essential to maintaining good posture here. You can run in the deep end for no impact, or in waist- or chest-deep water for a low-impact workout. (Try using the "Run tall" cue from p. 33.)

Workout: Descending Ladder
Warm-up: 10 min. easy
3 × 3 min. at tempo with 1 min. recovery
4 × 90 sec. at interval with 1 min. recovery
4 × 60 sec. at interval with 45 sec. recovery
3 × 15 sec. at sprint with 1 min. recovery
Cooldown: Easy swim for 5 min. Slide down into kiddie pool if available.

Use this pace guide to gauge your effort for pool running workouts:

Easy run pace: 8–10 steps per 5 sec.   **Interval pace:** 12–14 steps per 5 sec.
Tempo run pace: 10–12 steps per 5 sec.   **Sprint pace:** 15–16 steps per 5 sec.

Swimming

This fantastic no-impact activity works your whole body. Swimming can be exhausting when you don't know how to move efficiently through the water, so a lesson or two on technique is recommended! Vary your pace and effort depending on your fitness goals. Thanks to the no-impact perks of the pool, you can push your engine harder, more frequently, with less stress on your chassis, and leisurely swims make for effective active recovery.

Workout: Hundos

Warm-up: 50–100 yards of breast stroke and drills
8 × 100 yards with 15 sec. rest. Work up to 1600 yards total
Cooldown: Do a few laps with a kickboard or alternate strokes.

Cycling

Biking is more than a fun way to get around town; it promotes fast turnover and builds aerobic and anaerobic capacity with low impact.

Workout: Steady as She Goes

Warm-up: Core routine
20–90 min. easy-to-moderate-effort ride with smooth, high cadence
(fast turnover)
Optional: Stop halfway for ice cream or a cold drink.

Yoga

Yoga provides many benefits for runners, including breathing practice, mobility and flexibility, core and balance work, and mental focus. Some styles of yoga are harder and more taxing than others. With hot or faster-paced flow yoga, one session is enough activity for the day and might even make you sore. Yin, restorative, or other slower-paced sessions can complement other activities you do in a day and won't need recovery afterward; try them after running or other crosstraining if doing both in one day. All you need to practice yoga is a mat or nonslippery surface. You can find yoga routines online or go to a local studio for inspiration and guidance.

For Melody, a Kundalini yoga practice has strengthened her mind-body connection, and has been a powerful tool before races. For example, at the 2012 World Mountain Running Championships at Loon Mountain, New Hampshire, she leapt into a positive mental state and energized her body doing "Breath of Fire with Lion's Paws," which has a powerful, immediate effect on the brain. After five short minutes doing this on the riverbank, she was ready to "claw" her way up the mountain to a solid second place, making the team at age 38!

MOBILITY AND FLEXIBILITY: WORK IT OUT

Foam-rolling and other forms of self-massage can feel good before or after running and other exercise, before bed, or whenever you have a few minutes to spare. Using a foam roller, lacrosse or tennis ball, or stick-type massager, gently roll over—or just ease your weight onto and hold—sore or tight spots, such as calves, hamstrings, quads, glutes, and midback. Don't roll over joints, like knees, and there's no need to roll so hard that you bruise yourself.

Stretching is a relaxing way to cool down after a run and restore balance and can be an enjoyable ritual with teammates. Always stretch gently, never to the point of pain. Go to the point of the first, slight sensation, hold, and breathe for at least 30 seconds, then release. Focus on your calves and lower legs, quads, hamstrings, and hips.

WRITING PROMPTS

When I run, I feel

When I sit still, I feel

My favorite workout

Think of a time when you didn't feel like running but did, or when
you didn't feel like taking a day off but did. What happened?
How did it feel or go?

4

ADAPTATIONS

ZOOM IN ON PROGRESS AND GROWTH

There are lots of reasons to run and race. One main point of training and competition is to make progress. What does progress mean to you? For each athlete, it might mean something different. Depending on your perspective and season, progress may mean staying healthy, running faster times, getting bigger wins, setting personal records, finishing stronger, demonstrating grit, exercising consistently, or taking a break to recharge. Generally, it means improvement, maintenance, or recuperating, both physically and mentally.

Progress hinges on specific adaptations. Those adaptations include being able to run farther and faster, with more confidence and ease, plus other specific physical and mental wins. A bunch of factors affect your training, your recovery, and resulting adaptations. At first, you may make big, rewarding leaps quickly—the running fitness and learning curve is steep. After a while, and during some phases, though, progress will be less obvious. Know that is OK and part of the process. No running journey is a straight line up. Ideally, the top of your running curve will rest on a strong foundation that you've built with hard work and smart recovery over time.

No matter where you are in your journey, you'll inevitably hit some bumps, including injury, illness, and puberty. Think of them as pit stops—times and places to slow down, reassess, and refuel. Trust us: You can ride all of these obstacles out. In fact, with the tips in this book, you'll be stronger for them.

In this chapter we'll look at the adaptations that runners seek through training. We'll also explore factors that influence what adaptations, and maladaptations, like injuries, occur.

TRAINING ADAPTATIONS

When you add rest and recovery to stress and work, *tadah!* You gain adaptations. That means improvements in significant factors like endurance, speed, and freshness. Technical terms for markers of adaptations that enable you to run farther and faster, with more ease, include *aerobic fitness*, *lactate threshold*, VO_2max, *speed*, and *neuromuscular development*.

Let's look closer at these adaptations and what kind of workouts or efforts target them.

AEROBIC FITNESS

Your aerobic system, which delivers and uses oxygen, determines your endurance—how far and long you can run and involves your heart and lungs (remember, too, that when you're young, your heart and lungs are still developing). Your aerobic system also plays an important role in general fitness, maintenance, and active recovery. Easy running helps you build capillary beds, mitochondria, and the rest of the oxygen-transporting and oxygen-using system to increase blood flow to your muscles. Target this adaptation and you'll be able to run longer at higher intensity with oxygen as your fuel.

Aerobic training is relatively easy. It is slower and includes recovery jogs, training runs, long runs, steady efforts, and some moderate efforts. If you're focused on middle- and long-distance events, the bulk of your training should be in this zone. Events from 800m and up primarily rely on your aerobic system.

One of the best parts of aerobic training is that it can be social because you can talk! Talking helps you gauge your effort and work level too. At moderate efforts (the high end of your aerobic zone), talking will be harder—you might only be able to say a few words at a time. At the easy, lower end of this zone are conversational paces. (See Closer Look: Measure your work with effort levels, p. 31.)

Including a long run approximately once a week is an age-old running practice to boost aerobic fitness. After a long run, even if it's yammer-easy (aka long, slow distance, or LSD), it's best to wait approximately 48 hours before another quality effort to allow your body to recoup. Overall, aerobic training can make up three-quarters or more of your total running volume.

LACTATE THRESHOLD

As intensity increases, so does a substance in your body called lactate. Training at this higher intensity—often called tempo or threshold pace—teaches your muscles to efficiently metabolize lactate, ideally delaying the dreaded booty lock (you know, that feeling when you run an all-out effort and turn into the Tin Man with a cramped tush?). This effort is about 85 percent of your max heart rate, and it should feel like a 7 out of 10, effortwise. You should be able to say a sentence or two at the beginning and a few words at the end of the workout. Depending on where you are in your season, one workout in this zone per week suffices.

VO$_2$MAX

VO$_2$max is a measure of the maximum amount of oxygen used while working hard. Some fancy tests assign a VO$_2$ number, which age, genetics, biology, body composition, and altitude affect. What's most important is how well your body takes in, transports, and uses oxygen. You might cringe when your coach assigns workouts to target this (e.g., hard intervals), but know the tough sessions deliver aerobic *and* anaerobic perks. They require very high effort, and talking may feel impossible. This work is not all-out, like a full-on sprint, but is similar to the pace you could run in a 10-to-15-minute race. Runners and coaches tend to overemphasize this effort because it can get you fit, fast. But when VO$_2$max efforts are used as shortcuts or they take up more of the training pie than necessary, injury is bound to eclipse your whole pie. In the scheme of training, you don't need a lot of this work to find progress—about once a week when you're in season is beneficial.

SPEED

Speedwork can take many forms. For example, did you know running hills is speedwork in disguise? Whether short, fast, or long, hills help improve your speed, form, and efficiency without as much stress as running fast on flat ground. (Sneaky!) On flat ground, strides and repeats are examples of running work that can help improve running economy, aka how efficiently you run, and prepare you for faster speeds. Repeats in this sense are fast, but not a sprint. Run your repeats at about mile race pace, staying relaxed. Top-end speedwork is all-out—think flys and sprints—and improves your power and velocity plus boosts your neuromuscular prowess. These efforts should include long rest periods. Some training plans include speedwork year-round. In-season, race-specific speedwork may be done about once a week.

Stride it out

Strides are like the smartphones of training—they do a bunch of stuff at once, quickly! These short bouts of fast but smooth, relaxed running teach your body to go faster with less effort. They prepare your body for higher-intensity running, including races, and make your legs feel good after harder efforts. Try strides in a warm-up or cooldown, tacked onto an easy run, or as part of a workout. Optimally, they're included a few times weekly.

To run a stride, be sure you're warmed up. Then, take 15 seconds to accelerate to close to top speed, maintain for 10 seconds, then decelerate for 5–10 seconds. Stay as relaxed as possible and think *Smooth. Light. Fast.* Walk or jog until your heart rate is recovered before doing another, unless otherwise prescribed by your coach. Practice moving as swiftly and efficiently as possible.

Although all of this seems clear-cut, adaptations aren't quite so easily defined in practice. There are many blurry lines in training. Workouts designed to target one system might actually loop in several, while the aerobic system is essential for all of your workouts.

Many things can affect your pace, heart rate, and other indicators of training zones, adaptations, and recovery—weather, climate, stress, terrain, illness, for example. Pushing yourself harder isn't always better. Instead, work *smarter*. Remember to tune in to your body and practice deciphering its signals and your effort. There's power in those cues!

Your training should be guided by how you are responding to it. A coach can identify guardrails and determine what you're ready for: work, rest, or something in between. When in doubt—and not injured or in need of rest—go aerobic! Take an easy, conversational run with a teammate and do a set of strides. There's always something you can do to keep yourself moving forward, literally or figuratively. For example, making time for a nap can be a step in the right direction.

As long as you respect your body, prioritize recovery, run your hard days hard, and take easy days easy, then you will shine. Remember, you are developing. If you run with variety (mostly easy, some hard and fast), sleep a lot, fuel well, and have fun, you're going to get faster and stronger.

PERIODIZATION: BIG-PICTURE TRAINING

The pattern of stress and rest should be applied on both a short- and long-term basis. For example, zoom in on your week, and you may see a 7-to-10-day chunk of training: *Day off, easy day, hard workout, easy day, day off, long run, easy crosstrain.* Zoom out a little bit, and see a whole cross-country season: summer training, precompetition workouts, meets, sharpening, championships, recovery. Zoom out even further and see your full year: cross country, swim team, track and field, recovery, summer. Do you see how both stress and rest are built into your training,

---

Expand your horizons

PRO TIP

Training year-round as a runner boosts your running fitness, but did you know that training in another sport can have a positive effect on your running as well? Other sports and activities can increase your athleticism and durability, teach you a wide range of skills, and help you avoid burnout and injuries in your running season and career. Melody played basketball and softball when she wasn't running. Olympic marathoner Joan Benoit Samuelson skied. Pro Sara Hall played soccer. What other sports do you like to do?

from week to season to year? This idea of cycling your stress and rest on small and large scales is called *periodization*.

Thanks to the competitive seasons, running already has a built-in periodization. Take your foot off the gas after competitive seasons with breaks. Reserve your intense focus for special times of the year, such as six weeks of cross country and six weeks of track season. Do that, and you'll be able to floor it and fly past the competition!

WHEN INJURIES HAPPEN

Getting hurt is the worst. But the truth is the sport of running has a high injury rate, and you may find yourself injured at some point. It might be shin splints, knee pain, Achilles tendinopathy, or something else. Even if they're common, injuries can feel devastating.

> *The summer before I started college, my coach told me to run 60 minutes a day, so I did, despite a pain in my psoas. I didn't listen to my body. I needed a break, but I didn't take one. I didn't race a step for the Ducks that year, but I still wanted to run World Junior Cross Country Championships in Boston. So I kept training in the pool over holiday break. I still believed I could overcome injury and mountains of grief. I flew to the qualifying meet in Tennessee and placed third. But I ended up with another injury after that and couldn't go to world's.*
>
> —M.F.

Belief is powerful, as Melody's story shows, and you need it to achieve anything that's difficult, especially your dreams. It may allow you to race through an injury. But every body has a breaking point, as Melody's story also shows. If your body is too broken to move (or sit or sleep) without acute pain, then it's telling you to stop. Respect it. Because determination alone won't heal a crack in a bone. Hope won't untangle torn muscle fibers, not without a little assistance.

Instead, focus your belief on your body's ability to heal. Just as we give 100 percent to running, we need to give 100 percent to the healing process. Pro runner and coach Neely Spence Gracey says the best thing to do if you have an injury is to let it heal. You might be able to do some little things, she says, but don't go crazy with working out. In fact, trying to make up or keep up with a running schedule or season through cross-training can delay healing and cause other issues.

Melody was frequently injured in college, and it wasn't until she curbed her misplaced belief that she could run or train through anything that she was able to heal. When she turned her intense willpower toward taking a break from running and truly rested for a bit, she was able to strive again and hit her goals.

Depending on your injury, crosstraining may be a boon. But healing comes first. If you do choose to crosstrain, be sure that whatever activity you choose does not exacerbate your injury. Work with a PT, doctor, or other medical professional as well as your coach to coordinate an appropriate crosstraining schedule, including rest, and a return-to-running-and-racing plan. (For crosstraining ideas, see p. 49.)

WHY ME?!

Lots of things can cause a running injury. A sprained ankle can happen unexpectedly, for example. But often runners suffer from injuries with more complex causes. One example is overuse injuries. Often, these are a case of too much, too soon—drastic increases in mileage, intensity, or other training loads coupled with insufficient recovery. A lack of proper rest, including sleep, is another potential factor. And an unwillingness to be kind to and responsible for our bodies can make injuries worse.

Biomechanical factors may be at play too, but as you grow and develop rapidly during adolescence, those can be harder to discern. Growth itself can cause pain, as the term *growing pains* suggests! And then there are hormonal changes and nutritional factors that developing runners are vulnerable to. Injuries can also be signs of overtraining, burnout, and Relative Energy Deficiency in Sport (RED-S). In sum, a combination of external and internal details, including strength, flexibility, joint health, neuromuscular control, nutrition, and mind-body awareness, can influence whether (and how) a runner gets injured.

Your personality can affect your injury risk too. One study showed that runners who tended to be perfectionists were more likely to get injured. Perfectionists tend to push hard and ignore warning signs. Being stubborn, defiant, and determined can certainly be a strength, but it can also be a weakness. Those with a strong athletic identity also have a higher risk of injury. If you see yourself mostly as a "runner," then you may be more likely to train through pain; you might fear getting hurt or experience more distress when you do get hurt. While you are certainly a runner, remember you're more than that. You're a whole human! For many of us, running covers a lot of basic needs and wants—for example, fresh air, social connections, respect, acceptance, movement, and participation. Do you have other sources or ways to fulfill your wants and needs? Having a range of activities and support will make you more resilient.

Is it OK to run through pain?

Fleeting discomfort, some aches, muscle tightness, soreness, and fatigue are normal parts of training. But if you feel any of the following, stop, tell your coach, and see a medical professional:

* Sharp, stabbing, or acute pain, especially when it persists
* Pain that's a 4+ on a scale of 0 (none) to 10 (the worst)
* Pain that causes a limp when walking or alters your stride when running
* Pain that gets worse during or after running

Be especially tuned in to the following symptoms, two or more of which may indicate a bone injury:

* Pain after sudden or drastic change in training loads
* History of stress fracture, stress reaction, or repetitive bone stress injuries
* Low energy availability and/or chronic fatigue
* Pinpoint pain on bone
* History of dieting or restriction
* Weight loss
* History of irregular periods, late start to periods, amenorrhea, or other changes in cycle

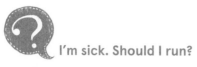 **I'm sick. Should I run?**

Probably not. Giving your body time and space to heal is beneficial for long-term development in addition to helping your body fight illness, says Megan Roche, MD, pro runner and coach. Especially if you have lung or digestive symptoms, it's best to nip whatever's ailing you in the bud.

Sometimes others—people in the running community or your parents or coaches—might prioritize your training and competition over rest and recovery, even when you're feeling hurt, sick, or tired. In many cases, though, running while you're injured or sick can make everything worse. It can make injuries last longer or recur or even cause permanent damage. Respect your body's cues so that you can run stronger over the long haul.

HOW TO DEAL

If you get hurt and can't run, you might feel isolated or stressed. Especially if running is your go-to coping mechanism, stress reducer, or social outlet. But being hurt can be a wonderful time to develop and strengthen new ways of coping with stress and other feelings. Here are some ideas: Start a daily journaling practice. Spend time doing nothing. See a mental health professional. Nap. Volunteer at an animal shelter. Go to movies with your friends. Prepare for the zombie apocalypse. Whatever brings you peace and joy as you recuperate.

OVERTRAINING

Feeling burnt-out, fatigued, or flat? You might be overtrained, which if unaddressed can progress into a syndrome. Overtraining can result from too much training, inadequate recovery, and/or low energy availability.

Melody experienced burnout during her freshman year of college after years of training hard. Grief over her mother's death, sky-high performance expectations, and loads of outside pressure all contributed to a tough phase. She had been injured all year and had yet to get her period. That's when she took a complete, much-needed break from running for a full three months as part of her year off.

Later, as a pro, Melody raced at the US Olympic Marathon Trials. When she didn't make that team, she chose to keep pushing to qualify in the 10K. But within two weeks of training, she felt drained, with no energy. Her heartbeat was irregular, and she felt low motivation and a heaviness inside. "I felt I *had* to qualify. There was not a sense of choice," she recalls.

Those negative feelings were a red flag. Being overtrained can steal the motivation associated with goals that once made you smile, so be aware of your workload. If you find you are losing pep in your step or don't feel like running anymore and have to force yourself, talk to your coach. Limit yourself to easy running, and add extra rest or extra fuel.

You might be exercising compulsively, which can lead to overtraining and complications, if you answer yes to the following questions. If so, please talk to your coach, a health care professional, or another trusted source about it.

> Do you ignore sharp pains?
> Do you keep injuries secret?
> Do you take painkillers regularly?
> Do you ignore the advice of your coach, doctor, or PT, particularly if they say to stop running?
> Are you tired all the time?

> Are you frequently sick?
> Are you feeling sad or depressed?
> Are your times and race performances tanking?

When it comes to training, remember that more is not always better. Countless details influence how—or whether—you grow and progress as a runner. Rather than forcing it, pay attention to what's actually going on in your mind and body, with help from info in this book and asking for guidance when you need it.

WRITING PROMPTS

A training log is a priceless tool when it comes to your running experiment of one. You can note your training, other stressors, recovery, and specifics like times and results. These details plot your progress over time. Writing in a log helps you keep track of the clues your body and mind are sending you, plus it can reveal patterns that affect adaptations. For example, tracking your period alongside your training reminds you to prepare for your body's rhythms and responses during specific times in your cycle. What else do you want your training log to include? Here are some ideas:

Date

Activity

Time

Distance

Description

How'd it feel?

Any pain or injuries

Period and hormonal symptoms

Shoes and gear

Other notes (concentration? mood? energy? weather?)

ᴍʏTRAINING LOG

April 3 ★★★★ ½ day!

TRACK, 4pm
1.5 mile w.n. jog w/middle-distance team
Dynamics + 4 x 100m strides
WO: Intervals with half interval distance recovery
   shuffle jog (heart rate stayed up but I managed :)
      800: 2:55
      600: 2:04
      400: 78
      200: 34
4 x 150 — Float, fast, faster!
1 mile cooldown + 2 laps barefoot, infield   (5 mi. total)

Stoked to be with the fasties
My strength work from winter is paying off.
I feel fit, not sharp—it will come!

★ First week of cycle, so this workout worked.
  Niggling calf strain—a non-issue.
  Used my racing flats—breaking in calves for spikes.

5

RUNNING WITH HORMONES

HOW TO TRAIN AND RACE YOUR BEST
THROUGH PUBERTY AND PERIODS

Puberty might cause a plateau in the traditional markers of running success. Why? It's a major rite of passage in your life. Your body is developing quickly and asking a lot of you.

Puberty is also when girls face extra hurdles. Society—including friends, peers, and adults—drops harsh judgments about how you look, what you do, and how that fits into cultural expectations. This might challenge your body image, your confidence, or your gender identity. And that's on top of a boatload of physical and mental development you're experiencing! Awkwardness and lack of discussion about puberty, and the periods it brings, add to the potential stress.

Whew, deep breath! You *will* emerge from puberty intact, with resilience, patience, and wisdom. The path may be bumpy, with lots of dips and snot-rockets. But if you're nice to your body, stay healthy, and keep moving forward, your running journey will carry you through puberty and take you to beautiful places.

Learning to read your body and mind's signals, without criticism, guilt, or shame is especially important during this time. This skill is essential not only to succeeding in running over the long haul, but also to navigating the physical, mental, emotional, and social whoop-de-whoops of growing up. When you honor your body, this phase is a gift—a call to hone your intuition and trust the process—that will enable even more progress down the road.

There's still tons to learn and discover through scientific research on female athletes of all ages (because unfortunately studies on and by women have lagged in most fields). But preliminary research and experts in endocrinology, sports medicine, nutrition, and more offer valuable insights and tips that can help you navigate your own cycles—they might even become a true superpower!

In this chapter, we'll discuss how to train, race, and weather the hormonal phases of puberty and periods.

TRAINING DURING PUBERTY

First, a refresher. As we talked about in Chapter 2, puberty is a massive growth spurt in more ways than one. Puberty affects balance and coordination, plus moods and feelings. No wonder it also affects your training, recovery, and subsequent adaptations. This is an especially important time to work smarter, not necessarily harder. Here are seven tips for training during puberty that can help you emerge stronger.

Emphasize aerobic conditioning. Low-intensity activity builds and maintains base-level fitness and promotes circulation, plus it relieves stress on the body and mind. Focus on your base mileage by logging easy, conversational miles and/or crosstraining, such as swimming, cycling, or other sports. Coaches should be able and willing to tailor your training to what's happening with your body.

Track your period. It might take a while for your periods to get into a rhythm. Recording your cycle and symptoms can help you figure out what's normal for you. Use an app or training log to track your period, recording flow (heavy, light), any pain (cramping, migraines), and factors like mood, sleep, and energy level. Note any unusual changes from month to month. While irregularities aren't always serious, they may indicate health issues; bring them up with a doctor (see p. 24 for specific symptoms to watch out for).

Keep your energy levels steady and balanced. Not having enough fuel (energy from eating and drinking) can delay your first period and cause serious health complications along with decreased performance. Remember to fuel not just for running, but also for your body's daily functions, all the growing you're doing, and other activities. Prioritize pre- and post-workout snacks to avoid energy deficits. (See Chapter 8 for some smart, tasty snack and meal options.)

Address food and body issues. Puberty, and cultural expectations around it, can have negative effects on your body image and eating habits. Stay alert. What messages do you hear about your body from parents, from coaches, or when you talk to yourself? What about from what you see online? How do these messages make you feel? Think, talk, or write about these influences. Practice mindfulness (p. 87) and use nutrition tools (p. 135) to help avoid dangerous traps. Seek help if you're struggling. In Chapter 9, you'll find information and strategies that'll help see you through the double whammy of diet culture and myths about runner bodies.

Build your athleticism and strength. Incorporate resistance training, crosstraining, and plyometric exercises to increase power, strength, and fitness. (You'll find great ideas in Chapter 3.) Multidirectional activities help build bone density, increase core stability, and improve explosive movements. Embrace other sports too!

Invest in a good sports bra. During puberty, you'll grow physically, which requires adjustment. Case in point: boobs, which might hurt or feel wonky when you run. A well-fitting sports bra can be a lifesaver (pp. 197–200 have sports-bra shopping tips).

Speak up. Yes, puberty is a big deal but it's also a natural process. There's no need to hide it under the rug—even if some people don't like to talk about it or periods. Talk about what you're dealing with or wondering about to teammates, your coach, or another trusted, supportive resource. If you're open about it, you might inspire others to speak up too.

RUNNING WITH A PERIOD

Hormones alter our bodies in many ways. They affect our energy systems, how we handle heat and regulate body temperature, our ability to gain strength and recover, and even injury risk. Woof! That sounds like a lot! But with a little self-awareness, you can actually tailor your training and lifestyle to these changes, from month to month, season to season, and year to year.

Even better, you can perform—and perform well—no matter the phase of your cycle. In fact, you can hit personal records (PRs) on your period. Paula Radcliffe set a women's marathon world record, 2:15:25, on her period, with cramps!

Your experience may differ from your teammates'—that's natural. For example, some people never deal with cramps but struggle with insomnia. Others get stomach troubles and break out like clockwork

GO WITH THE FLOW

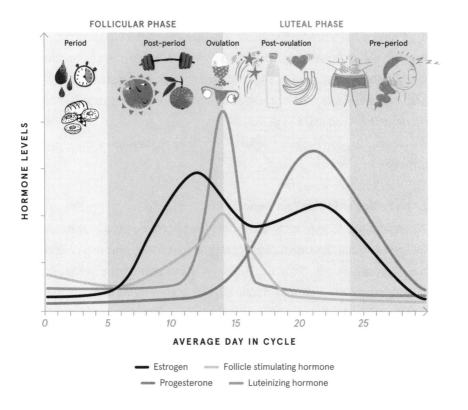

AVERAGE DAY IN CYCLE

- Estrogen
- Progesterone
- Follicle stimulating hormone
- Luteinizing hormone

every month. Having a strong sense of what's going on with your own hormones and their symptoms can help you as both an athlete and a human. Understanding your body invites you to give yourself grace, adjust nutrition and sleep, and work out and recover smarter. That's why we recommend tracking your cycle, including your own unique signs and symptoms. Knowledge is power! Most important? Your experiment of one. Here we'll share insights gleaned from experts and research, with some tips you can try, but you get to learn what works best for you.

Let's look at the whole cycle more closely. Once your menstrual cycle settles into a rhythm, it lasts about a month, with a week of bleeding, on average. The menstrual cycle has two halves, with ovulation in the middle. The first half is the *follicular phase*, and the second is the *luteal phase*. And those each have their own phases as well. Why? Because hormones fluctuate between and within each phase of a cycle. Their peaks, valleys, and plateaus—and ratios between the hormonal landscapes—may influence how you feel and perform.

Here's a rundown of the menstrual cycle, its phases, and some symptoms you may notice.

1. The Follicular Phase: Your period

When you "bleed," your body sheds the lining of your uterus, thanks to a release of chemicals called prostaglandins that make your uterus contract (*Hey-o*, cramps!). They also influence inflammation and immunity. During this phase, you may notice slightly higher blood pressure, feel some aches and pains, and might get sick more easily.

Despite all that, the hormones estrogen and progesterone are at their lowest during your period, which primes you for strong athletic performance! Even though many women suffer from cramps and bloating during their period, low hormone concentrations make it easier for you to use your muscle's carbohydrate stores, tolerate heat, mentally focus, and react more quickly, says Stacy Sims, exercise physiologist and research scientist. Melody remembers running a hard interval workout on her period in college feeling as bloated as a hot air balloon. But her stride was powerful, and she nailed the workout!

Since your cognition and coordination may be extra sharp, this phase is also an especially opportune time for skills, drills, and strength training (but don't skimp on warming up).

Period gear

When it comes to "feminine hygiene" products, you've got choices. As with shoes and other gear, what works for one person might not work for another. Experiment and go with what's most comfortable for you. None are fail-proof, but while leaks might feel mortifying, know that they happen to everyone with a cycle, even while racing!

* **Pads and panty liners:** These are easy to use, but might not be the most comfortable or leak-proof while running.
* **Tampons:** Some people have difficulty inserting them, but if they work with your body, they're a solid option. They come in a range of sizes and absorbencies.
* **Period panties:** Absorbent underwear is available in a range of styles, including leak-proof shorts.
* **Menstrual cup:** This little cup requires finagling to insert but offers a sustainable option.

When your period is painful, exercising can help, even if you don't quite feel like it. Exercise releases feel-good endorphins, and research shows that it fights symptoms. Moderate-intensity exercise is best; even a brisk 15-minute walk can be effective. Naproxen (Aleve) or acetaminophen (Tylenol) can help reduce pain too.

Blood loss during your period, especially if you have heavy menstrual cycles, can lead to high mineral losses. Focus on foods rich in iron, magnesium, and zinc, such as beans, spinach, whole grains, meat, and dark chocolate. Boost your body's absorption of these minerals by eating them with foods rich in vitamin C, such as strawberries, citrus, kiwi, bell peppers, broccoli, and Brussels sprouts.

2. The Follicular Phase: Between your period and ovulation

After your period, estrogen rises to a peak and progesterone stays low. You might feel energetic, happy, and more alert, thanks to hormone shifts. Your blood sugar levels may stabilize, your appetite may decrease, and your blood pressure might drop. You might even find an extra gear to push yourself harder or farther, and yet recover faster. Woo-hoo!

Depending on where you are in your season, take advantage of your power and energy levels peaking, and embrace more intense workouts and strength training. There is some evidence that lax joints during this phase increases risk of ligament and tendon injuries (such as in the knee), so that's another reason to warm up well and not skimp on cooldowns and mobility work.

Even when you feel like Superwoman, it can take 48 to 72 hours to recover from intense training sessions. Factor in rest days even when you're feeling stellar, and prioritize sleep to support your training, reduce injury risk, and maximize recovery.

Support your body by drinking enough fluids throughout the day and by eating vitamin C–rich foods with fuel that's high in collagen or collagen-building nutrients, such as fish with skin, bone broth, gelatin, and pumpkin seeds. Fuel with carbs before your workouts, especially those high-intensity sessions. To promote recovery, eat a post-workout snack with protein and carbs ASAP after harder training (try a DIY Smoothie, p. 150).

3. Ovulatory Phase

Two other hormones, called follicle-stimulating hormone and luteinizing hormone, spike. This triggers ovulation, when an egg is released for fertilization. That marks the halfway point in your cycle. You might feel amazing, or you might feel symptoms similar to period pains. Your heart rate might also increase, whether you're resting or running. Either way, this phase only lasts about a day!

4. The Luteal Phase: After ovulation

Estrogen and progesterone rise until before your next period. High hormones may disrupt neurotransmitters, including the "sleepy" melatonin and "happy" serotonin. So you might have a harder time falling and staying asleep, and notice changes in concentration, alertness, mood, or performance. Immunity may take a hit during this phase too.

You may also notice stronger emotions. Empathy, joy, and sadness might bring on the tears, and that's OK. Emotions are normal, and crying can help them flow.

You might feel warmer with an initially elevated body temperature. It may take longer to sweat and cool down. Sip on cold or slushy drinks during the day and while training to lower your core body temperature. Although higher hormones might decrease your thirst, make a point of replacing fluids lost from sweating with water and electrolytes. You might feel hungrier too due to increased resting metabolism, higher overall energy needs, and unstable blood sugar levels. Cravings are legit!

During running sessions, you may feel like you could run farther or longer, thanks to an endurance boost. Or you may notice higher heart rates and breathing. Depending on your season schedule, perhaps try to increase the distances and quality of moderate-intensity sessions. If your energy dips though, try lowering the intensity of your workout.

During this phase, high estrogen levels make it harder to use the carbs stored in your muscles, so it might be tougher to hit desired times during intense training. When you have high-intensity or 90-plus-minute aerobic sessions planned, try taking in carbs during the workout—try gummy candy, Smarties, glucose tablets, or dates.

You may notice your peak power is lower, so when strength training, reduce reps or weights as needed, which will give you the same benefit and optimal recovery.

Now is a good time to work on mobility and flexibility, and to get as much sleep as possible to boost immunity and promote recovery. Don't forget recovery days so you can adapt to all your hard work—especially because high progesterone can cause muscle breakdown. That's why it's extra important to focus on post-workout recovery snacks (with protein and carbs) within 30 minutes after intense sessions, plus protein-rich meals and snacks through the day.

Fight blood-sugar dips with that protein plan, plus complex carbs (whole-grain toast, PB&J, popcorn) throughout the day. Include fats and oils (nuts, seeds, nut butters, avocado, olive oil, full-fat dairy), which are essential during low- and moderate-intensity training and in light of higher estrogen. Finally, eat antioxidant-rich foods (fruits and veggies).

5. The Luteal Phase: Pre-period

Buckle up! When an egg isn't fertilized, progesterone and estrogen fall, triggering an inflammatory response, which could mean some pain and discomfort. For up to seven days before your period, you might feel stomach cramps, back pain, leg cramps, sore breasts, bloating, diarrhea, headaches, tiredness, mood swings, increased hunger, lower motivation or energy, or other symptoms (which may be diagnosed as premenstrual syndrome, or PMS).

Training might feel particularly hard during this phase. But any exercise can boost your mood and circulation and, therefore, may make you feel better. For example, yoga and Pilates have been shown to reduce PMS symptoms. Even if you would rather curl up into a ball under a blanket with Netflix and ice cream, a short walk, jog, or other gentle exercise is worth a shot. Mindfulness practices, sleep, and exposure to bright light help too. Stress levels can exacerbate symptoms, so practice saying no and relax when you can.

Try fueling with a variety of nutrient-dense foods during this phase. During training, your body adjusts its main fuel source, relying more on carbs. To support this—and blood sugar levels, cravings, and recovery—choose a well-rounded diet with antioxidant-dense foods rich in fiber, like fruits and veggies, nuts and seeds, and whole grains, plus protein sources including eggs, meat, dairy, soy, and fish. Fuel that's rich in iron, magnesium, and zinc with vitamin C–rich foods, as mentioned above, can help you get ahead of mineral losses from your period.And melatonin-rich foods (tart cherry juice, red grapes, bananas) may encourage sleep. To boost serotonin, try seeds, peas, legumes, soy, eggs, and whey; to target mood, try branched-chain amino acids, which are found in protein-rich foods like red meat and yogurt.

If you struggle with painful breasts or bloating during your period, try more electrolytes or adding a little extra salt to your food to reduce fluid retention.

What if I'm taking the pill?

Types of birth control, including oral contraceptives like the pill, vary widely. So do medical reasons for taking them. Those that include hormones come with their own set of symptoms and cycles. For example, a combined pill has estrogen and progesterone in it and produces a withdrawal bleed but masks your natural cycle. If your period is MIA or irregular, taking the pill isn't a simple answer or solution; research suggests it is not as protective for bones as once thought, and new research highlights other potential options. It's important to work with a health care specialist who's up on the latest research and can help monitor the pros and cons for your situation.

The key takeaway? A period is not simply a pain; it's a natural, healthy process and an important part of life. Know that your own experience of your menstrual cycle—including symptoms and responses to food, training, and recovery—is legit. And remember that although you might not be able to, say, change the date of a race, you can adjust your approach and mindset. A wise coaching adage says to prepare for everything and assume nothing.

I still remember feeling the increased size and density of my bones and the thickness and new curls in my hair when my period commenced. Hormones were transforming me and I loved it! My timing was good: I was in the middle of a year off when it happened, so I was able to be present in my body and not push through, something I'd become very good at doing, to my detriment.

I loved the feeling of growing. Being told repeatedly in high school how "light" and "waiflike" I was, as if it were a good thing, felt imprisoning. I was proud to embrace the "new" me, who embraced growth on all levels. —**M.F.**

WRITING PROMPTS

What I've heard about puberty

As I grow

When it comes to my period

6

A WINNING MINDSET

YES, YOU CAN HANDLE PRESSURE
AND MEET YOUR GOALS

What do you think about when you run? Do you talk to yourself? Do you sometimes get scared or anxious? Do you ever dread workouts or fear racing, or are you more likely to get amped up and excited? Do you pay attention to how emotions feel in your body and the thoughts that run through your mind?

Did you know you can change what goes on in your brain? Yep, your mind can learn to handle situations differently and rewire feedback loops. With careful mind and body training, you can become tougher, more resilient, focused, and calm—whatever you need to unleash your potential as an athlete and human. In fact, many of the world's best athletes use mental training to up their game. It just takes practice.

In this chapter, we'll cover the mental side of being an athlete, including growth mindsets, mindfulness, goal setting, visualization, emotions, and mental health.

A GROWTH MINDSET

During her first year at college, Melody wanted to run—and to be a champion—but injury, overtraining, and grief stopped her. She craved connection with others but at the same time felt shame for not maintaining her intense focus on training and racing, which had been her trademark in high school. Juggling all of this drained her, both emotionally and physically.

> *I needed to find happiness again. I followed the advice my mom had given me before she died and took a year off. I left campus, returned to Colorado, and stopped running while I worked several jobs, trying to make ends meet. The break from running allowed my hormones to flow, and I got my period. When I returned to Oregon a year later, I brought with me a growth mindset, instead of denial. I made room for mistakes and took the time, as written in* The Velveteen Rabbit, *"to become." It was not until I regained my confidence, through living authentically, that I finally ran faster in college than I had in high school. But I did. And I won.* —M.F.

How did Melody make such a powerful change? With a growth mindset—a way of looking at the world that embraces change and finds inspiration in challenge. Rather than getting stuck in her ways or feeling threatened by setbacks, Melody instead found happiness by being herself. She pointed her nose in the direction of where she wanted to go, figuratively and literally. She embraced the process of doing what she wanted—and truly loved—to do. That approach helped her meet her goals (and find success). What a gift, to chase dreams!

With a growth mindset, you are enough. You don't need to be over there where the grass is glinting greener or where Sally Swift is running

R.E.S.P.E.C.T.

Talk to yourself like you talk to your best friend—with understanding, patience, and kindness. This practice, called self-compassion, will help you stay motivated to overcome challenges big and small, such as grief or a workout that doesn't go to plan. Remember how the nervous system responds to stimuli from your inner and outer worlds? It's listening to the messages you send it.

---

20 × 400m or where you've lost five pounds. Perfectionism and comparison are thieves, stealing joy and compromising performance. It is only from here, now, that you can chase your goals. From here, now, you can just be! Be free to race, flail, run, and learn.

Let's dive into mental practices like mindfulness that can help you adopt a growth mindset.

MINDFULNESS

Mindfulness is a state of mind. It's about being aware of what's happening right here, right now. Not fixating on the past or worrying about the future, but instead being present and accepting it. It is a practice—an approach you can cultivate over time.

One of the perks of mindfulness is that it allows you to observe something in yourself or that is happening around you without being judgy or supercritical. It allows you to accept what's up—whether that's a thought, emotion, situation, or a feedback loop between those. For example, say you glance in the mirror before practice, smile, see some green leftovers in your pearly chompers, and think *Eek! How long was that spinach in my teeth?!* If you've been practicing mindfulness, you may avoid a spiral of shame and simply move on with your day. How? By

Hippo . . . what?

The hippocampus, a region of your brain, is involved in learning, memory, and emotional control. In a 2011 study, researchers found changes in this region and elsewhere in the brains of people who practiced an eight-week mindfulness-based stress reduction program, which included breath-focused meditation. That's powerful!

not criticizing, but rather simply noticing embarrassment or an overreaction to a little bit of vegetable.

Research suggests that mindfulness training may improve your stress responses and decision-making skills. So, it's helpful in running as well as life. For example, it can help you roll with being a second off a prescribed split or getting spiked in a race. As you observe and accept whatever situation you're in, you'll be able to handle it.

Mindfulness is a practice that you can try daily. One simple way to practice mindfulness is to *check in with your senses*. Do this right when you wake up, when you're bored in class, or when you're warming up at a meet. Ask yourself: What do I smell? Hear? Taste? Feel? See?

You can also practice mindfulness by taking *deep breaths*, anytime and anywhere. Tune in to your breath, a tool you always have with you: Can you hear it? Where is it going in and out of your body? When you pay attention to your breath, you're focused on the here and now. This calms your nervous system, especially when you take slow, deep breaths. Try it now: In . . . 1 . . . 2 . . . 3 . . . Out . . . 1 . . . 2 . . . 3 . . . How does that feel in your body? Know that deep breathing can actually change your state of mind!

Your brain is adaptable.
So are you.

Another tool for focusing your attention is using a *mantra*. Originating from Hinduism and Buddhism, a mantra is a word or sound repeated to aid meditation. Runners often use this practice in racing to bring their minds into the present. Melody's favorite mantras are *Smooth and strong* and *Allow (energy to flow)*. Try those or find your own mantras, such as positive phrases like *You can do it* or *Let's go!*

As you practice mindfulness exercises that bring your attention to *right now*, you might notice your emotions and thoughts more clearly. You might be able to respond more deliberately. You might act with a touch more control, rather than knee-jerk reacting without patience or intention. For example, you surge as someone moves to pass you. You bounce up after tumbling to the track and quickly regain your stride. You're resilient, bounding back from blips.

GOAL SETTING

How big are your dreams? What do you dare to imagine? Melody dreamed of going to the Olympics. Dreams open you up to possibilities. Goals set the course toward those dreams.

Setting goals requires looking up the road. While focusing on the present with mindfulness is important, thinking about the future is also essential, especially for athletes. Goals can motivate and guide the actions you take today and tomorrow, and that makes looking ahead to what's next even more exciting.

Planning for the future while staying grounded in today is not always easy. But remind yourself that focusing on now—and the small steps that need to be taken today—is what feeds the future. It's like lassoing a star. When you're connected to a sparkling, faraway goal, you have to hold on to the rope down here on earth.

Research shows that if you have positive expectations—for example, if you think you'll break 5, 6, or 7 minutes for the mile—you're more likely to do it. Sure, sometimes you'll stumble, fall, and maybe fail. But setbacks and missteps are part of the process. If we lassoed and wrangled in every starry goal on our first try, we wouldn't really grow or improve. We'd get bored! Disappointment is part of the journey; "failure" is essential for growth.

Coaches can help you dial in your goals. Ideally, goals are specific, short- and long-term, and challenging, but reasonable. Goals come in a few shapes and sizes. Some goals hinge on results ("I will win"), while others focus on process ("I'll do core work three times a week") and progress ("I'm shaving 4 seconds off my mile time").

Setting smaller, realistic goals—those that are a stretch but within the realm of possibility, such as doing a dynamic warm-up before every run—sets you up for success with bigger goals. Those little steps compound over time, until all of a sudden you look up from your path and see that you've connected with that star and you're running at a level that once seemed out of reach.

Reevaluate your goals throughout the season. Having a variety of goals, with a flexible strategy and approach, can make running more fun and rewarding.

Remember: Running is about progress and adventure, not perfection. Progress doesn't just mean getting faster. What progress means to you will change throughout your running journey. So pour your energy into your goals, but practice self-love all along the way. Results will come, one way or another, and they don't define who you are as a human.

SETTING S.M.A.R.T. GOALS

How, exactly, do you go about setting goals? One tried-and-true way is to make S.M.A.R.T. goals. The acronym stands for specific, measurable, attainable, relevant, and time-oriented. Use this template to figure out how you can turn a daydream into reality with a clearly-defined you. Try brainstorm-writing S.M.A.R.T. goals in your training log or journal.

SPECIFIC: What do you want to do? What are the small steps that will help you get there?

Example: I want to race at the cross-country state championship. To qualify, I will place in the top three at the district meet. To get ready to qualify, I will train consistently with my teammates.

MEASURABLE: How will you measure the outcome and track your progress?

Example: I will toe the start line and cross the finish line at the state meet. I'll place first, second, or third at districts. To train, I will run four days and strength train twice a week.

ATTAINABLE: Is the goal realistic? What support and resources can you use?

Example: I placed in the top 10 at districts last year and have been healthy, so this is a good stretch for me right now. I will talk to my coach, trainer, and teammates about this. I'll need their support to stay healthy and practice racing this season.

RELEVANT: Why do you want to accomplish this goal? How does it fit in to your values and your life?

Example: I love running and want to push myself. I'm proud of the way I have practiced working hard and facing tough competitors together with my teammates. I'm ready to devote time and energy to this new challenge.

TIME-ORIENTED: When and where will you complete this goal?

Example: The state meet is the first weekend of November. The qualifying district meet is the week before. Practice starts in two weeks, and that's when I'll start training consistently.

An inspiring team activity is sitting down together to brainstorm, write, and share goals. Melody led a team discussion at her university's preseason cross-country camp before her senior year. They all agreed they wanted to win their conference championship and regionals and place top-four in the country. Not only did this goal-setting session set Melody's course, it lit an amazing energy among teammates. (That year, the Ducks won the Pac-10 Championships and West Regionals and placed fifth at the NCAA cross-country championships by a close margin!)

TRAIN YOUR BRAIN

Mindfulness and goal-setting are two great skills for developing a winning mindset. But there's more. Mental practice is as important as training your body. (Because, ICYMI, your mind and body are connected!) Mental training makes running, competition, injuries, and daily life more enjoyable, tolerable, and rewarding. Honing your mental skills takes time and sometimes even professional help.

Don't wait until right before your championship meet to work on your mental game. Mental fortitude won't appear overnight. But it doesn't take years of practice to see improvements. One study on gratitude journaling showed that it took just eight weeks for folks to change white matter in their brain. And it takes 10 seconds to focus on a slow inhale and exhale, which has an immediate effect on your heart rate and muscular tension. Take mental training one step at a time, working up from basic mental skills (think: mindfulness, setting goals, repeating mantras) to more complex skills, such as visualization and managing emotions.

VISUALIZATION

Seeing yourself in action in your mind, a practice known as *visualization*, is a powerful tool. It lets you rehearse potential scenarios you might face in competition. Visualization prepares you for specific challenges, for example, racing under the lights or tackling hills with strength and poise. The practice has played a role in many athletes' success.

How exactly do you do it? First of all, prior to visualizing, it can be helpful to write about the scenario you'd like to focus on. (Check out the writing prompts at the end of this chapter for cues.) Then find a comfortable, quiet spot to sit or lie down, and close your eyes. Bring yourself into the present, where athletes must be to perform their best, with a deep, slow breathing warm-up. Take 8 seconds to inhale, hold your breath for 8 seconds, then exhale for 8; repeat this three times.

Next, picture the scene. Notice what you feel, using your senses, and see the details in your mind. If you're working on approaching hills with confidence, see the hill in front of you. Feel the cross-country course underfoot (grass? mud? concrete?) and hear your competitors around you (heavy breathing, swishing shorts, yelling spectators?). Feel your body—relaxed and strong, with a smooth stride—approach the hill with confidence. Look a meter or two ahead of your feet and hit the slope gracefully. Feel your arms swing methodically, feel your legs building heat but moving efficiently. Keep the rhythm going as you crest the hill, catching a little air before accelerating down the back side with ease.

Run through the scene until it feels familiar. Once you're done, take three deep breaths and slowly open your eyes. You can practice this daily or every few days, especially as you get close to a big race.

I first began using visualization to prepare for races in my sophomore year. I used piano music—George Winston's December album—to bring a racecourse to life in my mind. I listened to it every day for at least two weeks before a race. I would lie down, close my eyes, and see myself running every step of the race, examining details of the ground under my spikes and the features on the edges of the course, including race banners and spectators. The undulations, my breathing, the cadence of my feet rose and fell with the pace of the piano keys. —M.F.

HANDLING EMOTIONS

What happens when you're angry? Do you feel hot or clench your fists? Do you yell, stamp your feet, scowl? Do you get in trouble for the way you act when you're angry? Or do you even let yourself feel anger?

We get mixed messages about what we "should" or "shouldn't" do when we're angry—or feeling any emotion. Those mixed messages complicate matters and can sometimes even make us feel worse.

People might expect you to always be happy or agreeable. They might tell you to "calm down" when you're mad. They might not like what you do when you're angry or feeling another strong emotion. And that might cause you to feel shame about the way you feel.

But here's the thing: Anger is an emotion, not a thought or an action, and it's nothing to be ashamed of. What you *think* when you feel angry is a thought. What you *do* when you feel angry is an action. For example, imagine you're mad at your little brother because he keeps pestering you, and when he won't stop, you think *Ugh! He's got it coming!* and punch him. Socking him was your reaction-action. It's what you decided to do with the anger you were feeling.

Punching your brother will probably get you in trouble (duh). But getting angry shouldn't. Anger is just one of the many emotions you will feel in your lifetime. And it's not a "bad" thing. In fact, it can actually help you when you're running, if you know how to channel it.

Moderate levels of anger can help you go faster or give you more power and motivation. Too much anger, though, makes it hard for your brain to work effectively. For example, if you're in a race and someone elbows you in the ribs, and you get mad and punch her like you punched your brother, you'll get disqualified (DQ'd). Reacting aggressively is definitely not the way to run your best race.

To harness anger—or to process any emotion—you need to get to know it. This brings us back to mindfulness. When you start to feel the cues your body is giving you—including signs from your nervous system—you can learn to decode what emotion you're feeling. This will help increase your "emotional intelligence," aka how smart you are about your emotions and those of people around you. As you work on mindfulness, and as you grow up, you'll figure out the best ways to deal with anger before it piles up and, well, you punch someone. Ideally, you will learn how to acknowledge it—and all your emotions—without judgment and, if needed, channel it into motivation, movement, or another expression.

Many athletes call in experts to help manage emotions and learn mental skills. One tool in the psychology realm is cognitive behavioral therapy (CBT), which trained mental health experts use to help people not only cope with mental health issues like depression but also with sports-related stress. It's a method of identifying your thoughts and using a skills-based problem-solving approach to them, says Dr. Marilou Shaughnessy, a clinical psychologist. It can be applied in a range of situations to fight anxiety and improve self-talk and focus. If, say, an athlete is feeling extremely nervous when thinking about an upcoming race, a therapist might interrupt and say, "Hey! Stop! What were you just thinking?" and then help you figure out how to handle it. You can try a CBT-style approach on your own as well. Practice questioning what you're thinking about and asking yourself how it's connected to emotions or sensations you're feeling in your body.

CBT is just one tool that can help increase awareness and mental health. Others include mindfulness exercises, breathing practices, and journaling about your thoughts. These practices and tools, whether done with a professional or on your own, can help you get to know how your brain acts before, during, and after practice and competition. Bonus: Athletes who strengthen this mind-body connection find benefits not only in sports, but in the rest of their lives too!

Sometimes emotions creep up on us. You might not even realize that you're super stressed. That is, until you've yelled or cried or felt overwhelmed. You might dismiss or try to ignore these unpleasant sensations or other stressors, but know that they matter. Because *you* matter. And what you feel matters. Give whatever you're feeling your (kind) attention.

Talking or writing about what's bugging you can help relieve pressure. When you're feeling stressed, overwhelmed, or depleted, try a *tantrum journal*. It gives you an opportunity to get your thoughts out of your head, which clears space in your mind for other things, like an upcoming workout or race. This activity, created by Kelsey Griffith, a mental skills specialist, is especially helpful if you don't know, exactly, what the heck is going on or why you feel upset.

HOW TO TANTRUM JOURNAL

1. On a blank piece of paper, quickly write down everything that's on your mind: What are you thinking about? How do you feel? (Stressed? Mad? Sad?) Why? What little or big things are piling up? (Homework, headache, doubt, pressure from coach or parent?)
2. Once the page is full, put down your pen and take a deep breath, in and out.
3. Read what you wrote.
4. Flip the page over and title it "To Make It 1 Percent Better." Write down one to three things that you can you do to make it 1 percent better. Can you take your day one chunk at a time? Can you tell your parents or coach how you feel? Can you take a nap or ask for an extension?

Can you be OK with your race time if you give it your best effort? Can you give that feeling in your stomach some attention? Brainstorm positive thoughts and actions.

5. Take another deep breath. Now tear the page into little pieces, toss it into the recycling bin, and know that you have freed up space in your mind and will take everything one step at a time.

STRESS, DEPRESSION, AND ANXIETY

Chronic stress, depression, and anxiety are mental health issues. They aren't "just in your head"—they're related to your environment, genetics, and sometimes trauma (like abuse and harassment). What's more, they are common and serious. You should not ignore these illnesses. They can be treated with the help of tools like therapy, stress management techniques, medications, and support groups. That's why it's important to speak up if you're suffering and ask for help when you need it.

I had never been depressed before, but I knew something like it was happening during my freshman year. On bad days, it felt like I was wrestling a giant octopus that hovered over me. It taunted and slapped me around with its heavy, solid arms. Once I shook the first one off, then a left hook and a jab followed, and a whack from the back that knocked the wind out of me and sent me stumbling to the safety of my room. I was exhausted from battling this darkness and craving anonymity and peace. —M.F.

It's natural to feel stress—such as before a test or race, or if your teammate jumps out of a bush to scare you. This kind of stress is actually beneficial and kick-starts hormones that help you react to what's happening around you. But repeated or ongoing stress can lead to chronic stress, which piles up. Sometimes it coincides with other illnesses, such as depression (feeling persistently sad or hopeless) and anxiety (feeling strong fear or apprehension). Chronic stress can hurt performance, too.

How do you know you're overstressed? Your body holds clues. Here are some signs that you might be too stressed:

> Headaches and body aches
> Light-headedness
> Depression (persistently sad, empty, hopeless, pessimistic, irritable, guilty)
> Anxiety (worrisome, fearful)
> Stuttering
> Getting lots of colds or illnesses
> Fatigue

> Trouble sleeping and nightmares
> Upset stomach and GI issues
> Wetting the bed
> Sweaty palms
> Shaky hands

If you're experiencing signs of stress, first of all, remember that it's a normal human response. We all feel it in response to what's going on in our lives, minds, and bodies. While this chapter offers tools you can practice to help you cope, those tools don't always work and aren't enough to treat mental health illnesses. So talk to a trusted parent, coach, friend, or health care professional about how you feel and take steps to get treatment as needed.

When we're feeling overwhelmed, even saying how we feel out loud helps us identify and cope with feelings, fears, or worries. Some of our best warm-ups, cooldowns, and long runs have included sharing our scary feelings and deepest, darkest secrets with trusty teammates. Maybe they asked open-ended questions or called us out about a funk or foul mood. Maybe they just listened. No matter what, they were there for us. (And those teammates became some of our best friends. Forever. The sisterhood is strong.)

A winning mindset is not simply "thinking happy thoughts." It's about tending to your mental, social, and emotional health. The mental skills and practices are about focusing on what you can do and on what you can control, rather than on what you can't. They take practice. You *can* harness the power of productive thinking and a growth mindset.

Treating your thoughts (and your whole self) with care and compassion is not only good for you right now, in the present, but it can also help motivate you to improve down the road. (Remember Melody's year off?)

As with little bits of stress, little wins add up. So keep working your mind. Figuring out how your puzzle pieces fit together is a challenge, but it's also pretty fun. Mental skills training can help you learn to work with—and even control—your mind. Among other benefits, that control can help you feel OK whether you win or lose. An important lesson for life, as well as for sports.

Are you or someone you know struggling with mental health issues?

Seek help from a trusted adult or healthcare provider. If you or a teammate is showing any of the following signs, reach out immediately for help. The National Suicide Prevention Lifeline provides 24/7, free, and confidential support for people in distress, prevention and crisis resources for you or loved ones, and best practices for professionals. Call 1-800-273-8255 or visit https://suicidepreventionlifeline.org.

Warning signs

* Talking about wanting to die or wanting to kill themselves
* Looking for a way to kill themselves, like searching online or buying a gun
* Talking about feeling hopeless, having no reason to live, being trapped, or in unbearable pain
* Talking about being a burden to others
* Increasing the use of alcohol or drugs
* Acting anxious or agitated, behaving recklessly
* Withdrawing or isolating themselves
* Showing rage or talking about seeking revenge
* Extreme mood swings

Many mental health struggles are tied to trauma, including sexual violence. In fact, one in nine girls experience sexual abuse or assault by the time they are 18. Anyone affected by sexual assault can find support on the National Sexual Assault Hotline at 1-800-656-HOPE (4673). Visit http://online.rainn.org for support via confidential online chat.

Mental health struggles may also be related to eating disorders, which we discuss in Chapter 9. The National Eating Disorder Association has a free, confidential helpline (1-800-931-2237, http://myneda.org/helpline-chat) and 24/7 support via text (send NEDA to 741-741).

WRITING PROMPTS

Ten things I can't stop thinking about

Ten things I'm grateful for

Visualization: Sketch out a scenario to rehearse in your mind.
For example, write about responding to someone trying to pass
you, or standing on the line with confidence, or finishing strong.

What does the scene look like?

What do you smell, hear, feel, or taste?

How might this feel in your body?

What steps do you take?

THE JOURNEY OF WOMEN'S RUNNING
A TIMELINE

Women's running has reached amazing heights. More girls and women are running—and running faster and farther—than ever before. But it hasn't been a smooth journey.

Humans started running about two million years ago, likely picking up the pace to follow prey or to escape from predators. Running is natural, an act born of survival. It might be hard to fathom—using nothing but your body to get around—but we are built to run, and to run far!

Eventually, humans ran to communicate, celebrate, and pray. Many cultures around the world include women in rich running traditions, such as those of indigenous Native Americans. In Navajo and Hoopa tribes, running is part of women's coming-of-age ceremonies. In ancient Greece, women created their own religious festivals, in which runners wore their hair down and knee-length tunics slung over a shoulder, leaving one breast out in the breeze.

But societies have stopped women from running or organizing their own sports and questioned women's athletic abilities. In 1899, for example, physical educators created an association that enforced strict rules for girls and women in sports. For more than half of the 20th century, athletic opportunities for girls and women were severely limited. The few track clubs that sprouted up were squashed (often by those who deemed competition unladylike).

In the US, many of the first girls and women who ran were ridiculed, harassed, and ostracized. They were told they'd turn "into men" and that their uteruses would fall out. They were turned away from—or forced to sneak into—races. The closest that Olympian Doris Heritage Brown came to competing for her high school track-and-field team was riding the bus with the boys to their meet. Girls were not allowed on the track! Kathrine Switzer, the first woman to officially enter and finish the Boston Marathon, was famously shoved by a race official during the race in 1967.

At the college level, women organized their own national championships. The first was held in 1969. In 1971, professors and coaches from around the country organized the Association for Intercollegiate Athletics for Women (AIAW), a governing body (on the heels of the Commission on Intercollegiate Athletics for Women) that initiated and organized sports for college women, with nearly 1,000 schools and a TV contract.

When a national law called Title IX was passed in 1972, it said that any program that uses money from the federal government has to treat all students equally. That includes schools and their sports teams. The National Collegiate Athletic Association (NCAA), which supported men's sports since the 1900s, fought a (losing) battle against Title IX. In fact, the NCAA shunned development of women's sports, write running historians Mike Hubbard and Jack Pfiefer. AIAW fought a (losing) battle against the NCAA, which eventually hosted its first championships for women's divisions—a decade later.

Title IX rules aim to level the playing field for girls, ensuring the ratio of teams reflects the student population and creating opportunities for female athletes. But rules only work if people follow them. Some schools still don't give girls equal opportunity to play sports, according to the National Women's Law Center. Some girls, especially students of color, have even fewer sports opportunities and lack access to athletic resources. In elementary and secondary schools in the US, boys get more chances to play and compete in sports. They also have more access to coaches, better places to practice, and even higher-quality gear. Plus, the sports industry and coverage are predominantly male: coaches, leagues, owners, reporters. So, too, lags exercise science and medical research on female athletes. Whether you want to go pro or be a fan, the reality is we still face uphill battles.

Despite all that, women runners have made impressive progress and are chipping away at old ideas. It's important to celebrate how far we've come. Waves of pioneers have carried women's sports forward. They've organized competitions, broken barriers, spoken out about injustices, and generally kicked butt. The opportunities available to you today are thanks to generations of runners who've come before you. Here's a look at some of those pioneering athletes plus key milestones along the way.

776 BC

Ancient Olympics includes a men's only 600-ish-foot race. Women organize separate competitions.

1882

First women's athletics games held at a YWCA in Boston.

1896

Women barred from competing at the first modern Olympics, but at least one woman ran the marathon anyway.

1900

Amateur Athletic Union (AAU) and International Olympic Committee (IOC) allow 22 women to participate in a limited number of "feminine" sports, including croquet, at the Olympics.

1920

International Women's Sports Federation starts women's games, the first large-scale opportunity to participate in track and field.

1922

Women's World Games held in Paris.

1928

IOC introduces limited women's events at the Olympics, including an 800-meter race, inaccurate coverage of which sparks backlash.

1954

Diane Leather breaks 5 minutes for the mile, running 4:59.

1960

Women's 800-meter race reintroduced to the Olympics. Women race in five different running events, and teenager Wilma Rudolph sweeps the sprints.

1963

Merry Lepper runs a 3:37:07 marathon, one of the first women to officially finish a marathon in the US.

1964

Wyomia Tyus wins first of two gold medals, becoming the first person to win the 100-meter race in consecutive Olympic Games in 1968.

1967

Kathrine Switzer finishes the Boston Marathon, despite attempts to force her off the course.

1969

First collegiate track-and-field championships for women hosted in Texas.

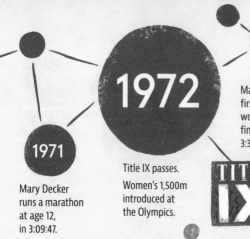

1971

Mary Decker runs a marathon at age 12, in 3:09:47.

1972

Title IX passes.

Women's 1,500m introduced at the Olympics.

TITLE IX

1973

Marilyn Bevans, the first African American woman to officially finish a marathon, runs 3:31:45 in Baltimore.

1974

Judy Ikenberry wins AAU's first national marathon championship for women.

1983

Mary Decker wins 1,500- and 3,000-meter events at the first track-and-field world championships. (She was later suspended from participation due to a drug test, which she contested.)

1984

Joan Benoit Samuelson wins gold at the inaugural women's Olympic marathon.

1985

Zola Budd sets 5,000-meter world record on the track running barefoot.

1987

Sports Illustrated magazine cover features its first woman track-and-field star, Jackie Joyner-Kersee.

1 2 3 4 START

25803

2003

Paula Radcliffe sets world marathon record (2:15:25 in London), which the international governing body (IAAF) recognizes separately because she raced with men.

2008

The 3,000-meter steeplechase is introduced as an Olympic event for women.

2013

Mary Cain places second in the 1,500-meter race at the USATF Outdoor Championships and, at 17, is the youngest woman to make the IAAF World Championship finals.

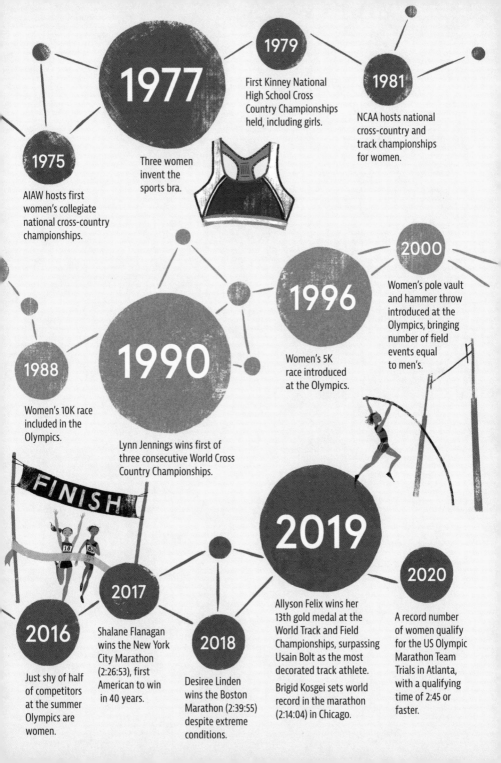

1977

1979 First Kinney National High School Cross Country Championships held, including girls.

1981 NCAA hosts national cross-country and track championships for women.

1975 AIAW hosts first women's collegiate national cross-country championships.

Three women invent the sports bra.

2000 Women's pole vault and hammer throw introduced at the Olympics, bringing number of field events equal to men's.

1996 Women's 5K race introduced at the Olympics.

1990 Lynn Jennings wins first of three consecutive World Cross Country Championships.

1988 Women's 10K race included in the Olympics.

2019 Allyson Felix wins her 13th gold medal at the World Track and Field Championships, surpassing Usain Bolt as the most decorated track athlete.

Brigid Kosgei sets world record in the marathon (2:14:04) in Chicago.

2020 A record number of women qualify for the US Olympic Marathon Team Trials in Atlanta, with a qualifying time of 2:45 or faster.

2017 Shalane Flanagan wins the New York City Marathon (2:26:53), first American to win in 40 years.

2018 Desiree Linden wins the Boston Marathon (2:39:55) despite extreme conditions.

2016 Just shy of half of competitors at the summer Olympics are women.

FINISH

7

COMPETE LIKE A CHAMPION

TIPS AND STRATEGIES FOR RACING FIERCE

Runners, take your mark . . . Set . . . Go! Do those words give you goose bumps? Butterflies? Cause your heart to pound? Make you smile from ear to ear? Racing is integral to running. It's also one of the best things about our sport. When it comes to competition, Melody likes to say, "Always have hope in your heart and wings in your heels." Racing gives you the chance to go for it—to see what you are capable of—whether with runners or against the clock. Maybe you'll surprise yourself. Maybe you'll break a barrier!

In this chapter, we'll talk about competition and what comes along with it, including emotions and expectations, race-day routines, performance strategies, and running competitively in college.

RACING

Standing on the start line might bring about nerves, but they're the kind that flutter like butterflies when something's exciting. After all, racing is an incredible privilege. It's a fleeting moment in which we get to explore limits, face demons head-on, and dive headfirst into the now.

"The thing I find most thrilling about racing is every single time I toed the line, I was a mixture of confidence and self-doubt. It didn't matter whether it was two laps around Fresh Pond in Cambridge, Massachusetts, an all-comers run every Saturday . . . or whether I was standing on the starting line at the Olympics in 1992," says Lynn Jennings, one of the winningest US runners ever, who won bronze in the Olympic 10K and won the IAAF World Cross Country Championships three times in a row. Racing matters because it's a triumph over our self-doubts, she says.

Competition might feel intimidating or even scary, but the truth about racing is that there will always be somebody faster than you, and someone slower than you—if not now, soon enough! Understanding and accepting this takes pressure off being "the best." So if you're worried about rankings when you stand on that starting line, remind yourself: *Even if I am the fastest or slowest one here today, another day I might get beaten or win because that's how it works. What matters is that I try now.*

Trying—that's it. Racing is an experience, one that teaches you about yourself, regardless of what the numbers on the clock say. It doesn't define you or your worth. "It's a snapshot. It's not a character indictment if you don't win or if you fall short or have to stop for a minute to breathe. That's just who you are today, and tomorrow you will be another version, the next version of yourself," Jennings says.

There will be hills, weather, and myriad obstacles. How will you respond? Will your feet callous and toughen? Will your legs fly? Will your heart shine bravely? For pro runner Neely Spence Gracey, one race experience in particular delivered an epiphany. The World Cross Country Championship course in Poland was daunting, with mud, hairpin turns, and steep hills. Gracey knew she was likely to fall down, lose a shoe, or get tossed around. But she was determined to run her own race one step at a time. She asked herself, "Am I running the right race for me right now?"

Gracey's perspective at that race changed everything for her as a pro, and not just because she was the top American finisher. That day, she says, she learned how to race. "It's about my goals, my preparation, and how I show up," she says. "I make the most of the race, of myself on that day."

Pro runner Allie Kieffer holds another perspective. "I go to a race, and I feel like I can beat anybody," she says. "When I go to the starting line, it's like a fresh slate, an opportunity." Kieffer also asks herself what's the worst that could happen. If she runs a time that is slow compared to her previous races, she uses it as a starting point for the next phase of her training.

RACING AS A TEAM

Racing, especially in high school and college, is not solely an individual endeavor. While you may have individual goals, your team likely has goals too. Running with a team is an amazing experience. When you put on your school's or club's singlet, you're representing your community. Your singlet is a reminder to you and your teammates to work together, to support and push each other to explore limits, hopes, and dreams. Singlets also remind us we're stronger together.

In cross country, for example, every runner can count, if not score. If the seventh runner on your team passes another team's fifth runner on the homestretch, she's made a difference in the final score. Pack running is a racing strategy where a team's runners stick together as long as possible—not only to place higher, but to displace other team's runners.

Whether your team is going for the W, trying to best a rival squad, or simply attempting personal records (PRs), you and your teammates can lift each other up. This is something you can bring to other races further along your running journey. Whether you're in a club or racing solo, competing means *with*—not just against—other people.

CLOSER LOOK

Points!

Cross-country and track-and-field teams compete for the best scores at meets. Here's how to tally points:

Cross country

* The team with the lowest score wins. That's right, the lower the better.
* The top five runners on a team score points.
* First place earns 1 point, second place 2, third place 3, and so on.
* The best possible score is 15, if a team's top five runners place first through fifth. (This is called a perfect score.)
* Any runner can make a difference in the overall score.
* In high school, teams may divide their roster into varsity (the top runners), junior varsity, and sometimes freshman squads, which each compete in separate races.

Track and field

* The team with the highest score wins.
* High school competitions may include 16 or more events (running, jumping, throwing, and combined) in which athletes can score points.
* Scoring depends on the type of meet and the rules of the host, including how many finishers score and whether relay teams earn extra points. Examples:

    Dual meets (against one other team):
    First place earns 5 points, second 3, third 1, including relays.

    Invitational meets (against multiple other teams):
    First place earns 10 points, second 8, third 6, fourth 5, fifth 4, sixth 3, seventh 2, eighth 1.

> *Championship meets (the big meets at the end of the season against your town or league, district, regionals, and/or state): First place earns 10 points, second 8, third 6, fourth 5, fifth 4, sixth 3, seventh 2, eighth 1.*

* Competitions sometimes come down to the last event, the 4 × 400m relay. That's why you should stick around to cheer teammates on even if you're not racing!
* Athletes can compete in multiple events. This is a sport where participation at meets really matters.
* In high school, a team may be divided into varsity, junior varsity, and freshman squads, which may compete in separate races or events, or even separate meets.

RACE-DAY PREP

Race day is just another day. But let's face it, it's a day with a little extra excitement. Perhaps there will be mud or cheering or a number pinned to your top! Whether you're racing cross country, track, or another race, you'll find it easier to get into a groove by using some reliable prerace routines and rituals. Here are tips to keep in mind:

> Eat and drink well leading up to the race so you're glycogen-full and hydrated the moment you step on the line (see Fueling around Exercise: Preworkout/Race, p. 141).

> In the days before the race, pick a mantra (for example, *Strong, strong, strong,* see p. 89) and practice visualization (see p. 93) so when race day rolls around, you can use both to get into the zone.

> Besides your team uniform, shoes, and spikes, choose your favorite, most comfortable gear, including at least one sports bra and a pair of socks.

> Do your familiar prerace warm-up from practice with teammates.
> Prepare for everything and assume nothing, including weather. Everyone else will be facing the same conditions. Remind yourself you can handle a little rain, or cold, or whatever Mother Nature unleashes. If it's hot, try prehydrating to fight sweat and fluid loss and consider shortening your warm-up. If it's cold, race with gloves, a headband, or other extra gear, and adjust your warm-up accordingly.
> If you get nervous, acknowledge it, as elite coach Lauren Fleshman recommends. For example: *Oh, hi nerves! You're a sign that this is exciting and that I care. Thanks for showing up, but I'm good and can take it from here.*
> Avoid your phone and comparison traps like rankings and top-time lists—that quicksand will sap your energy!
> Double-knot your laces.
> Listen closely to your coach and the meet announcer so you know when and where to check in with meet officials, warm up, and start the race.
> Cheer for your team, friends, and whoever could use a boost. (TBH it's all of us.)
> Remember: Have fun, with a focus! That's the point!

STRATEGY

Racing middle and long distances doesn't mean sprinting from the starting gun to the finish line. Melody likes to negative split (run the second half faster than the first). This is a common approach of world-class athletes. In both of Melody's Foot Locker Cross Country National Championship wins, she did not take the lead until after the first mile. This requires trusting your mental strength as well as your fitness.

To race well, it's important to learn to pace yourself. You can do this by practicing varying your effort in workouts or on easy to moderate runs. Pay attention to how you spread your effort throughout a session. You can also run without a watch or split cues to determine—by feel—the rhythm of your effort.

Pacing yourself is like making a peanut butter and jelly sandwich. Are you globbing spoonfuls of peanut butter on one side of the bread, or are you carefully spreading it across in an even layer? Once you add jelly, is your ratio to PB off, or is it balanced? Try testing out a few different approaches in practice. Worst-case scenario? You bonk or get booty lock (that cramping feeling in your rear and legs when you've run all-out). As long as you walk away with new knowledge and continued curiosity about how to build your most delicious PB&J sandwich, you're stronger for it.

Another key to good racing is to start out confidently. Get out quickly enough to get into a smart position without draining your immediate energy stores. Then progress into a rhythm, breathe, and as the adrenaline from the start wears off, remind yourself not to fall asleep. Instead, tell yourself it's time to get to work. Start moving up, allowing competitors and teammates alike to motivate you into getting the most out of yourself.

Once you've dialed in your pacing and start, work on making moves during races. Throw in a surge, challenge someone who runs up on your shoulder, stick with someone who passes you for 100 meters. The goal? Giving maximum effort—your very best—up until the split second you cross the finish line! Competition makes us dig deep.

No matter your goal or plan, make sure to keep your eyes and ears in the race in order to observe and react to what's going on around you.

I went to the World Cross Country Championships with the goal to win. My strength—focused tunnel vision—had obscured how the race was unfolding and I did not see two women break away. My strict prerace plans—A, B, and C—blinded me to other possibilities. I landed myself on the podium in third. —M.F.

Races rarely go as planned. Often they're filled with jostling, unexpected moves, and even falls. Here are tactics for tackling some of the challenges you might face.

Tight packs. You're going to get elbowed, possibly even in the boobs or kidneys. Be assertive. Protect your space. Learn how to stand up for yourself without being deliberately or unnecessarily rough; do not impede any competitor or you will get DQ'd. Activate your forearms. Make them like steel so when someone pushes against you, you are a solid barrier. Be fierce! Take up space!

Side stitch. If you tend to get cramps in your torso, try this prerace exercise: Lie on the ground. Bend your knees with your feet on the ground, hip-width apart. Place your arms out to the sides, relaxed with your palms up. Fold your right leg over your left. Gently drop your knees to the right, and turn your head to the left, allowing rotation to travel up through your spine. Inhale and exhale three times, as deeply and completely as possible. Take a fourth inhale and hold it for 10 seconds, then exhale forcefully, until all the air is out of your lungs. Switch sides and repeat. If it happens in your race, try to breathe into it and hang tough.

Falling. If you take a tumble in a race, pop up! Unless you're injured, use the surge of adrenaline that will course through your veins to regain your stride. Work steadily to find a new position. If you fall down frequently in practice or races, you might be tired or underfueled, in which case try taking a day off, drinking a milkshake, and incorporating single-leg and proprioceptive drills into your training. Also work on upper-body strength, ankle mobility, and lower-leg strength (see Chapter 3 for examples).

Getting passed. It happens. How will you respond? First, dig up that grit inside you—you've definitely got some—and resist the urge to slow down. Try to surge with the other racer. If they persist, as you are being passed, try imagining a rubber band (or hair tie or scrunchie) attached from your belly button to the center of the passing runner's back. Let it pull you along and hang tough!

Feeling tired, uncomfortable, in pain. Start with the idea that if you begin something, you will finish it. Accept that racing can be uncomfortable, searing, and sometimes even pukey. It makes us feel countless fleeting sensations. If you feel sharp or pinpointed pain, ask yourself if it is a damaging kind of pain. If it is, call it a day and take care of yourself. But if the pain isn't signaling an injury, remind yourself that it is there to chisel you, to develop your grit and resilience, and to test your determination and strength. Embrace it. Don't forget, the faster you run, the sooner it'll be done!

Going out too hard and bonking. Practice pacing. Be humble. Check your ego at the Porta Potty on the way to the start line. To avoid fading, start more conservatively (slightly slower) in the first third of the race so you can pass competitors later. But it's a balancing act, and the trick is to not go out too slowly. You want to use up everything you have to give by the time you stride across that finish line. If you're bonking because you're low on energy (signs include dizziness, lightheadedness, stomach grumbling, feeling weak), review Chapter 8, and eat more and/or more frequently, including more protein, carbs, and fat. Have a bigger snack or meal prerace (making sure to leave enough time to digest).

Tummy trouble. Stress, nerves, and running hard can cause us to sprint for the toilet or garbage can. Relax, this happens to most runners, whether they admit it or not! If you tend to experience GI distress before or during races, test out easier-to-digest prerace fuel (such as plain toast, bananas, white rice, or applesauce). If your digestive issues exist during normal training or when you're not running, see a doc.

Coming in last. If you gave your best and worked for every inch of the race, congratulations! No matter what, there's no place to go but up! Keep training, and focus on areas that need work, such as your aerobic fitness or your final kick. Incorporate fast strides, speed, and A, B, and C skips so that you can keep driving when called upon (see Chapters 3 and 4). Did you finish last because you gave up? Work on your mental fortitude (see Chapter 6).

Winning. *Woo-hoo!* Own it. Embrace it. Celebrate it. It's awesome, but know that it doesn't define your worth. Winning may bring with it some extra attention and pressure upon you or a sense of needing to live up to expectations. Acknowledge that, then take it one step at a time, knowing we all win some and we all lose some. Practice mindfulness to stay grounded (p. 87).

Criticism. Is your coach, parent, or brain hypercritical of your race? That can be a difficult experience. After your race, try to decipher what you are

Race-Day Gear Checklist

- Spikes with wrench and metal spikes or flats (for the race)
- Running shoes (for warming up, cooling down)
- Socks
- Sports bra (one for competing, one for after)
- Uniform (shorts, singlet, warm-ups)
- Water bottle
- Pre-race snack
- Post-race snack
- If cold: jacket, layers, gloves, warm hat, extra socks
- If hot: sunscreen, SPF lip balm, electrolytes
- Hair ties
- Tampons, pads, or other period gear
- Watch
- Mantra

feeling and how the race actually went. Competition makes you dig, and this includes digging deep for something positive about your race, even if it's just the fact that you showed up and crossed the finish line. No matter what, if you put effort forth, take pride in the fact that you uncovered new layers of yourself and gained fitness. Remember that there's a lot of value in putting yourself out there, pushing yourself and taking risks, no matter the result or what your brain or someone else tries to tell you.

COLLEGIATE RUNNING

Do you want to run in college? That's a meaningful goal for some athletes. There are plenty of opportunities to run cross country and track and field as a student at a college or university. Each opportunity varies, meaning that there's a wide range of experiences available. Don't assume that the most competitive or widely known school is necessarily the right fit for you. Do your research, and consider the following tips.

Many athletes hope for athletic scholarships. But, TBH, getting an athletic "full ride" (all the costs of college covered) is unlikely for most

How fast do I have to be to run in college? What times do I need to hit?

Time standards range widely by division and program. Some less competitive programs—smaller schools or divisions, especially those without athletic scholarships—might not have any at all. Some coaches look more closely at meet results, such as where an athlete finished at the state cross-country meet, than at times. While many collegiate coaches are focused on times to decide who to recruit, other coaches look for untapped potential and how much passion an athlete has for contributing to a positive team culture. Look at team websites to find out what times current athletes run. Reach out to a coach if you're interested or curious about what it takes to make it onto their team. And keep in mind that many schools also have running clubs—intramural or recreational groups—with which you can train and race, without many of the demands and high standards of "official" collegiate competition.

---

cross-country and track athletes. This is due to how the structure of the collegiate system, and each school's athletic department, is set up. Partial scholarships often require fast times, but you needn't necessarily hit those standards to "walk on" (try out for or join a team without being recruited by a coach of that program). Know that many collegiate runners get academic scholarships and need-based financial aid.

Before you start the college-hunting process, take the first important step: Figure out *why* you want to run in college. Do you enjoy being a student athlete now? What are the benefits and challenges? How do you add your fuel to a team fire? What do you like to do outside of sports? Use the questions and writing prompts provided in this chapter to help you define why you want to run competitively.

The next steps are all about organization and time management. You'll need to think ahead, prioritize your needs and wants, act professionally, and make a plan, says Cassandra Cunningham, coach and mentor to athletes. Her top advice? Do your research! "If you can find a place where you can succeed and fail, then you'll find joy and happiness, but you have to do your homework," she says. Here are some of the questions to ask as you consider if and where to run in college:

Questions to ask yourself
> Do I like being a student athlete? Why?
> Do I prioritize athletics, academics, or social life? Or do I try to juggle all of them at once?
> What intrigues me about running in college?
> Am I comfortable not being the fastest? Or being the slowest?
> How do I feel about more than one practice or workout a day?
> Are my running goals highly competitive or more laid-back? (e.g., Do you want to win an NCAA title or set personal records? How big of a leap would those goals require?)
> Do I prefer being a big fish in a little pond, a small fish in a big pond, or somewhere in between?
> What do I add to a positive team culture?
> What other goals or hopes do I have about college?

Questions to ask about a school and its running program
> What division is the school? Is it in a competitive conference or region?
> How big is the team?
> What are the coaches' goals and backgrounds? Do they have a winning record?
> What are the athletic standards and expectations?

- > What are the school's and team's academic standards and expectations?
- > How much time do athletes commit to the team, training, and competition each week?
- > What financial aid is available?
- > What academic, sports medicine, mental health, and nutrition services does the program or school provide to athletes?
- > What flexibility do coaches offer? For example, must all athletes compete in three seasons: cross country, indoor, and outdoor track? Can you redshirt (take a season without official competition)? Travel abroad? Have an internship during practice hours?
- > What do current athletes like or dislike about their coaches, team, facilities, and experience?
- > Do team members hang out together?
- > What happens if an athlete is injured? How many athletes are hurt each season?
- > What is the coach's training philosophy and approach to developing athletes as both humans and runners? (e.g., What mileage do freshmen run, or does it vary?)
- > How do coaches, teams, and the school support freshmen transitioning to college life?

WRITING PROMPTS

My first race

What happens when I run hard

Five things I fear and five things I enjoy about racing

When I think about my future and running

Being a student athlete is rewarding and challenging in these ways

8

FUELING FOR SUCCESS

HOW TO FEED YOURSELF AND YOUR BUSY LIFE

Opinions on nutrition are like noses. Everyone has one. We hear a lot about what, when, where, and how to eat and drink. And what, when, where, and how to *not* eat and drink. This information is confusing and contradictory and sometimes even wrong. That's why in this chapter we want to share validated insights about sports nutrition as well as basic guidelines for eating and drinking. The goal? Fueling yourself and your great adventures.

There's so much we could talk about when it comes to nutrition. As with other topics in this book, entire professions are devoted to the subject. It's best to see an expert—a registered dietitian (RD)—when you have questions and concerns. But if you are going to be successful with your experiment of one, you need to start on the right foot, empowered. (Especially because misinformation abounds!) We'll provide you with basic tenets of nutritional science—sourced from experts—that are particularly important for adolescent female athletes. And we hope to inspire you to fuel with both enjoyment and curiosity. (Spoiler: There's no perfect runner's diet!)

In this chapter, we'll discuss research-backed practices for eating and drinking as a young runner and growing human, equipping you to make choices that work for you. We'll also cover pre- and post-run nutrient timing and even dish up a few of our favorite recipes. *Bon appetite!*

FUELING FOR SPORT AND LIFE

Fueling for performance is important for your running, but fueling for your own nutritional needs *outside* of sport is essential. Most of the nutrition information you read online or hear from people around you is not specific to you, an athlete and young adult. It's all too common to underestimate the high energy demands of puberty and adolescence, let alone running. You may need more fuel than your parents or coaches or even some of your friends. This is because (a) you're growing; (b) you run; (c) you're super busy, juggling lots of activities; and (d) you're alive.

Food is the fuel you need to go, do, think, make, run, be. When you eat breakfast, a snack between classes, or a family dinner, you nourish your life. Your body breaks down what you eat into energy and essential ingredients. Sources of energy (called *macronutrients*) are carbohydrates, protein, and fat. Smaller nutrients (called *micronutrients*) include vitamins and minerals. In a given day, you could use more than 40 nutrients!

Fueling enough with a variety of nutrients allows your body to function, develop, work out, and recover from exercise and stress. Your body draws on different fuel for different exercise sessions. High-intensity interval workouts, for example, rely mostly on carbs; low and moderate efforts draw on fats and carbs. Long sessions—think over an hour—may benefit from you taking in carbs during the session. The levels of fuel you use depend on how long and hard you work out, plus your fitness level, and what you ate or drank prior to a session. (Not to mention that your brain needs carbs to think and study!)

Understanding how your body uses what you eat to help you do all the things you're doing every day, from running to studying to sleeping to growing, is a head start on prioritizing your well-being. Let's begin by taking a closer look at those major players in your diet—nutrients.

MACRONUTRIENTS

Carbs, protein, and fat play starring roles in your health, growth, and running. Here's how.

Carbohydrates

Carbs are your primary source of energy. Your brain, muscles, and liver love them. They can also be stored as glycogen, aka running rocket fuel. Carbs are especially important before and after you exercise because they provide efficient energy and kick-start your body's repair processes.

CLOSER LOOK

Don't complicate carbs

Carbohydrates are organic compounds made up of the elements carbon, hydrogen, and oxygen. They form sugar, starches, and fiber. Your body breaks down all carbs into sugars (glucose), which enter your blood. This triggers your pancreas to release insulin, which helps push sugar into cells that use it as energy. Your body stores sugar as glycogen in muscle and liver cells. Sugar molecules organized in long chains form complex carbs, which take longer for your body to break down than simple carbs. Simple carbs are easier to digest, which makes them useful for prerun fueling. That said, many runners swear by prerace oatmeal, considered complex.

You'll find them in grains, starches, fruits, and vegetables. Some carbohydrates are complex, including whole-grain and high-fiber choices, like oatmeal, with lots of vitamins and minerals. Other carbs are simple, such as refined and lower-in-fiber options, like white bread. These are easy to digest and quick to absorb.

Sources: *Bread, rice, pasta, potatoes, crackers, tortillas, cereal, apples, bananas, squash*

Protein

Protein is a complex compound that contains amino acids, which are building blocks for your muscles and cells. It's especially important for growth, recovery, and lean muscle mass. For example, it encourages recovery after hard sessions. You don't have to slam multiple protein shakes or a steak to get the benefits of protein. Spreading protein intake throughout the day keeps energy levels up and you satiated.

Sources: *Beef, chicken, eggs, Greek yogurt, cheese, beans, tofu, nut butter*

PRO TIP

Milking it

Cow's milk is a treasure trove of carbs, protein, electrolytes, vitamins, and minerals, and it's inexpensive compared to so-called sports products. It includes lots of nutritious perks, like calcium, phosphorous, B_2, and vitamin D (if it's fortified— good for your bones!) and protein, plus water, sodium, and potassium for hydration. Use it as a smoothie base or drink chocolate milk as a recovery drink. If you're sensitive to dairy, try lactose-free or A2 milk, or fortified soy milk.

Fat

Fat, an essential organic compound, is the third primary fuel and has multiple benefits. Slower burning than carbs, fat is satisfying and also helps you absorb vitamins and minerals from food. Research suggests it might even help protect against injuries. It's found in fatty meats and fish, plus nuts and oils.

Sources: *Butter, cheese, salmon, salad dressing, nuts, olives, avocado, chips*

MICRONUTRIENTS

In food, you'll also find small essential ingredients called micronutrients, which play important roles in your health. These include vitamins, minerals, and phytonutrients, beneficial chemicals including antioxidants. Let's look at some that are extra helpful for runners.

Calcium

Calcium is essential for your bones, particularly during the first two decades of your life, when your bone mass and density are developing. Calcium may also decrease the incidence of bone injuries, like stress fractures, and it plays important roles when it comes to running, including muscle contraction. Aim for 1,300 mg/day, which you can find in about three servings of calcium-rich foods.

Sources: *Milk, yogurt, cheese, tofu, cottage cheese, frozen yogurt, chia seeds*

Iron

Iron helps with metabolism and moving oxygen. It's found in red blood cells, in hemoglobin proteins that carry oxygen from the lungs to organs, muscles, and in other tissues. As a female runner, you are at risk for being short on iron due to loss through sweating, periods, growth, and the GI tract, and red blood cells breaking down more quickly because you're active. Some things affect how well you are able to absorb iron from your diet, including timing, caffeine, and calcium. Not eating meat or restricting food can also negatively affect iron levels.

Sources: *Red meat, pork, turkey, liver, shrimp, fish, eggs, apricots, prune juice, spinach*

CLOSER LOOK

Iron it out

Low iron levels are fairly common among runners, especially girls. Iron deficiency can affect training and performance because it lowers your ability to transport oxygen. Anemia, a condition, means there's low red blood cells. Symptoms include weakness, fatigue, declining performance, shortness of breath, dizziness, headaches, and even craving ice. If you suspect you have an iron deficiency, it can be diagnosed with a blood test. Ask for a ferritin test as well as the common panel. For athletes, ferritin levels of 40 to 60 and above are desirable. (That's higher than the "normal" lab test range.) If needed, an iron supplement can be helpful, but you should work with a doctor to determine the appropriate dosing. It can be dangerous to supplement, so do not take iron liquid or pill supplements "just in case." For those who need iron, research has shown that taking iron every other day may help absorption. Other tips: Consume iron with vitamin C-rich foods, without caffeine and calcium-rich foods, and not three to six hours after working out hard, as a hormone spike can hinder absorption. Iron supplements might cause digestive issues, so pair them with food.

B Vitamins

These vitamins are busy B's (see what we did there?). They help break down food and aid in growth and development. B_6, in particular, is important for oxygen transportation.

Sources: *Turkey, chicken, salmon, tuna, potatoes, chickpeas, whole grains*

Magnesium

This mineral helps with hundreds of body functions. For example, it helps muscles move, nerves communicate, and bones strengthen.

Sources: *Cashews, almonds, sesame seeds, bananas, leafy greens, dark chocolate, avocados*

SUPPLEMENTS

Supplements are extra: products consumed *in addition to* regular meals, snacks, and drinks. They include vitamins and minerals in pill form and so-called performance products. Many running-related nutrition products claim to help you before, during, or after exercise. They can be expensive and, TBH, you don't need running-specific gels, chews, drinks, or waffles to run fast or well. Basic whole foods (e.g., potatoes, bananas, or dates, sprinkled with salt) work as well (at lower cost) if not better than these shiny packaged options. But every body is different, so see what works for you.

Most sports dietitians recommend a food-first approach. That means aiming to get your essential nutrients and fuel from meals, snacks, and drinks. Generally, supplements are an unnecessary expense, and what's more, they aren't regulated like prescription medicines, so you can never be sure what exactly is in them. (Athletes sometimes fail doping tests for this reason.)

Eating mindfully

Melody's highest achievement in running, making the World Track and Field Championships in the 5K in 1997, was due in part to fully embracing "mindful eating." She made a point of making time to eat, of breathing while she ate, and truly enjoying the food she tasted. These are simple, but transformative, practices.

While eating, do you really taste your food? How many times do you chew before swallowing? Take note of how foods make you feel: Energized? Nauseous? Sleepy? Satisfied? Was the meal a relaxed or social event, or was it grab-and-go? Do family or team dinners feel more nourishing than eating alone? The point of noticing these things isn't to judge; it's simply to notice. Tune in to the experience of eating—all the data you gather is helpful in your experiment of one! Used thoughtfully, this data can improve your health and happiness. Let it help you honor your hunger, identify fullness, and discover satisfaction—which are components of Intuitive Eating, an evidence-based mind-body approach championed by nutrition experts.

In some cases, taking a supplement may be helpful to deal with specific deficiencies. For example, in the case of anemia, a doctor may recommend an iron supplement (see Iron it out, p. 130). Another supplement worth considering is vitamin D. If you aren't exposed to sunlight for at least 15 minutes a day between 11:00 a.m. and 3:00 p.m., a vitamin D supplement might help your bone health, among other factors. Check with your doctor and RD.

ENERGY BALANCE

Runners often ask registered dietitians to tell them precisely what to eat. RD Maria Dalzot won't do that. "You're not a machine or a robot. You're a

ENERGY
BALANCE

FUEL
ENERGY INTAKE

LIFE+ACTIVITIES
+TRAINING
ENERGY DEMAND

living, breathing human, and every day is different," she says. She says she needs to talk to an athlete for a while to get an idea of what's going to be helpful for her. That's because individual needs vary. Dalzot—who is also a professional trail runner—tailors her advice and recommendations to each athlete's scenario.

For these same reasons, calorie-tracking apps, online calculators, formula-based charts, and template plans are often inaccurate and even harmful. They leave a lot of holes. For example, they don't compute your hormones, your training, your culture or food practices, your recovery, your gut, your growth, your hopes or dreams! So let's throw those out now along with the scale and one-size-fits-all plans and advice.

The most important nutrition principle for runners is energy balance. Imagine that balance—aka how much energy is available to you—sort of like a playground seesaw. Your goal is to keep the seesaw level with enough energy to fuel your body's functions and all the things you are doing throughout your day. Your balance is wonderfully unique to you.

We know our bodies require a certain amount of energy *in* so we can put a certain amount of energy *out*. But how much? Well, let's see: You need fuel for (1) living, (2) growing, (3) running, and (4) other activities. When the energy you consume through food and drinks is sufficient to fuel 1 through 4, you'll feel good, run strong, and handle life like the boss that you are. Bonus: You'll also steer clear of serious energy-deficiency issues such as LEA and RED-S (see p. 159).

Your body is an incredible gauge of fueling and works with the many interrelated systems at play when you eat. In your gut, for example, there's a giant universe of microbes, microorganisms like bacteria that help with digestion, immunity, metabolic function, and even mood and brain functioning. Your brain is constantly listening to the signals your cells and organs are sending about energy stores, gut health, emotion, sleep, and more. Based on those deets, your brain creates signals that lead to the signs of hunger and fullness that you feel.

If you're training hard or are very busy or very stressed, your body's signals might get muddled or muted. Plus, it's easy to forget to keep your energy levels topped off. But know that fueling consistently and sufficiently—for your workouts and for your days—keeps your seesaw level and your body performing at its best. What you eat and when can make all the difference in your day, as well as in your adaptations to training and racing.

FUELING FUNDAMENTALS

First and foremost, there's not one "right" way to eat—phew! No food is inherently "good" or "bad." And "what so-and-so eats in a day" is a filtered snapshot, not a guide. Here are some other important basics to remember, provided by Megan Medrano, RD:

1. Eat enough for healthy living and fueling all that extra-important stuff like breathing, cell growth, and repair.
2. Eat enough to fuel and recover from running and workouts (so you can train hard and build your body up after you break it down).
3. Eat a variety of foods to get a wide range of micronutrients, including vitamins, minerals, and electrolytes.
4. Make it a point to eat all the macronutrients—carbohydrates, protein, and fat—throughout your day.

Maintaining your energy balance is an ongoing endeavor. You might notice signs of hunger popping up every two to four hours or increasing after a race or long training run. What your body requires changes on the daily. "Calorie needs are not stagnant . . . because what you do changes day to day," says Dalzot. Furthermore, our bodies themselves are constantly changing. So it only makes sense that our nutrition needs change as well, she says. If you have concerns, need specific guidance, or just want to know more, reach out to an RD (see p. 182) to ensure your fueling is tailored to you.

If you remember one thing about how to fuel, make it this: Fueling empowers you. Eating is your strength and your not-so-secret weapon for better recovery, better workout quality, and injury prevention!

READING THE SIGNS

As you get to know your own body and its signals, learn to trust it. Rather than looking at what other people are doing or eating or drinking, focus on what works for you. "Tune in to your hunger cues, your fullness cues, your recovery time," says Medrano. "If there are certain foods that you eat at certain times, and you feel like you bounce back more quickly compared to eating other foods, then that may be the meal that your body responds to best! Tune in rather than look outside yourself for a ton of resources."

Some days you might overeat, or you might undereat, or you might need extra snacks. That's OK! No matter what, keep listening to and learning from your body. Hone your ability to figure out what you want and need, whether it's carrot sticks and hummus while you finish your homework or pizza dipped in ranch with a group of friends or a post-workout smoothie.

Hunger is your body's built-in call for food, and it actively sends you signals that say "Feed me!" Remember that exercise can change these signals. You might get the first hint that it's time to eat by way of your

Signs that you might be underfueling

* Persistent injury
* Low energy that makes it hard to do things
* Not getting a period
* Your mood or motivation is in the toilet
* You keep getting sick
* Recovery takes forever
* Most running feels like junk
* Trouble concentrating
* Difficulty falling or staying asleep
* Waking up in the night feeling hungry
* Thinking about food all the time

mood or mind. For example, maybe you find yourself daydreaming about snacks or your attitude tanks or you get angry (aka runger). You might feel drowsy, notice brain fog, or simply smell food and want it! More urgent signs of hunger include light-headedness, difficulty focusing, headache, fatigue, and belly rumbles.

Don't wait until you're famished to eat. Rather, eating consistently and eating until you're satiated helps you avoid feeling starved. Plus it keeps your seesaw balanced and avoids the bonkers hullabaloo caused by LEA (see p. 161).

FUELING ON THE DAILY

Ideally, eating would always be delicious, relaxing, and among family and friends. But you're busy, and fueling isn't all organic produce rainbows. When you're in a pinch, any fuel is better than no fuel. Be sure to eat when you can and allow yourself to enjoy your food—even if that means taking two minutes to sit down and chew a Pop-Tart. Remember: Breathe.

PRO TIP

Snack attack

A Clif Bar, a Snickers, and a PB&J may come in different packaging, but did you know they offer nearly identical amounts of fuel, including protein, carbs, and fat? As RD Heidi Strickler notes, simply because something is "processed" or comes from a vending machine doesn't mean it will hurt you. Plus, just because a snack is labeled "performance" doesn't necessarily mean it is more nutritious or a better choice for runners. The point? Any of those choices could be a solid snack. And for the record, any snack is better than no snack.

As a baseline, RDs recommend at least three meals and three (or more) snacks a day for teen runner girls. They recommend including the three macronutrients (carbs, protein, fat) plus a variety of fruits, veggies, and fun foods; a calcium source at breakfast, lunch, and dinner; and combining several food groups for snacks.

Every runner's fueling needs are different, but here's a rough sketch of what a day of eating might look like for a high school cross-country runner. Nutrient timing is key for athletes, so we've included pointers for fueling your way from morning to night plus before and after harder efforts. Consider working with a specialized RD to ensure your intake is optimal.

BREAKFAST

A mistake many runners make is waiting too long to eat. In the morning, your body is ready to take in and use fuel, especially carbs, and a solid brekky will set you up right—and fight stress hormones (like cortisol) that spike in the morning. Kick-start your day with hearty, slow-release carbs and protein, plus water or another hydrating drink. Before you reach for caffeinated coffee or tea, though, read Coffee break (p. 139).

Examples

> *Overnight Oats (see recipe, p. 148) + an egg + fruit*
> *Breakfast burrito with eggs, cheese, veggies, and salsa + fruit*
> *Slices of leftover pizza or casserole*
> *Smoothie with yogurt, banana, berries, oats, PB, greens, milk or juice (see recipe, p. 150) + toast*
> *Cereal or granola with milk or yogurt and banana, mango, or frozen berries + toast + juice*
> *Toast sandwiches with hummus and avocado or nut butter and honey or jam + 2 eggs*

Coffee break

Some athletes use coffee as a prerace boost. Some students use caffeine—tea, coffee, pills—to stay awake. Should you? Although some studies suggest that caffeine might help improve race times and alertness, it has side effects, such as tummy trouble and sleep disruption. It's also easy to take too much and to get addicted—an expensive habit! For young runners, we don't think it's worth that risk.

LUNCH

During a busy day at school, it might be tempting to skip lunch. Don't! Not only is it a great time to catch up with friends and take a break, the midday meal also sets you up for a strong practice or competition later in the day and keeps your seesaw balanced.

Examples

› *Sandwich or wrap with tuna, chicken, egg salad, or sliced meat; veggies; and mayo, avocado, or cheese + carrots and crackers/chips/ pretzels with hummus*

› *Sandwich or wrap (1–2) with nut butter, jam/honey, and creative toppings (fruit, seeds, shredded coconut) + crackers/chips/pretzels + carrots + jerky + fruit**

› *Quinoa, chicken, veggie bowl with avocado or olive oil + trail mix + fruit*

*No fridge needed!

SNACKS

Snacks keep your energy levels up throughout the day. Sports dietitians recommend *at least* two to three daily snacks for adolescent runners.

You might notice a dip in the afternoon especially, so definitely plan for a midafternoon, prepractice snack. Make a snack by combining two to three food groups. Stash less-perishable items such as granola bars and trail mix in your locker or gym bag for backup.

Examples

> *Crackers and cheese*
> *PB&J sandwich*
> *Greek yogurt and granola*
> *Granola bar and berries*
> *Apple and trail mix*

DINNER

Dinner is another great opportunity to fill up on much-needed nutrients. Remember to include fun foods, like fries, ice cream, or cake, if you want them—no food is off-limits.

Examples

> *Rice and stir-fry with vegetables and chicken, shrimp, or tofu + milkshake*
> *Macaroni and cheese with tuna and broccoli + cookie*
> *Burrito bowl with rice, ground meat, beans, salsa, avocado, greens + chocolate*
> *Vegetable Beef Soup (see recipe, p. 149) + baked potato + salad with dressing + pie*

If you're hungry later in the evening, have a snack! After-dinner snacks can set your body up for better restoration overnight. To potentially help with recovery, try casein and whey protein (found in yogurt) and tart cherry juice, red grapes, or banana (which also include sleep-friendly melatonin—bonus!).

FUELING AROUND EXERCISE: PREWORKOUT/RACE

What you eat and drink before workouts and races may require a bit more planning than other days. Running hard diverts your body's attention (including circulation) from digesting to more important things, such as running fast, so it can be helpful to stick to easier-to-digest fuel.

You may have guts of steel, or maybe your digestion is more delicate. Your teammate may be able to scarf a chicken Caesar salad seconds before heading out the door for a long tempo workout, while your stomach can only handle a banana or energy bar so close to a workout. When Melody was in high school, her race-day fuel included snacks like Power-Bars, yogurt, poppyseed bagels, and salted, roasted peanuts.

What's the best prerace and preworkout meal or snack for you? Experiment! But something with carbs and some protein and/or fat is a good bet. FYI, some foods, like high-fat or greasy options (chicken tenders, for example) are tougher to digest, so aim for a snack that's easy for you to process.

Just remember to eat before you run, especially in the morning. Even a small snack can fight spiked stress hormones. Training and racing require unique nutrition, and it will take some trial and error to figure out what prerun fuel you like and does not cause digestive issues. (You might sacrifice a workout or two but that's no big deal.)

Here are some ideas for topping off your tank *before* harder efforts, depending on whether you prefer to eat a lighter or a heavier meal beforehand and the timing of your race or workout:

Larger meal (3–4 hours prerace or preworkout)

› *Whole-grain pasta + protein + cooked veggies*
› *Deli sandwich with protein + chocolate chip cookie*
› *Any of the Lunch options (p. 139)*

Lighter meal or snack (2–3 hours prerace or preworkout)

› *Toast or bagel with PB and honey or jam*
› *Sweet potato or baked potato with butter or coconut oil*
› *Cereal with soy milk or yogurt, erring on less fibrous side*

Light snack (to top off fuel levels, 1 hour or less prerace or preworkout)

› *Banana*
› *Energy bar*
› *Raisins or dried mango*
› *Toast, cracker, or pretzels*
› *Sports drink*

FUELING AROUND EXERCISE: POST-WORKOUT/RACE

After your race or workout is a critical snack time. Your goal? To rehydrate, repair, and replenish. Have a snack or a nutrient-dense drink within 30 minutes of finishing a harder effort.

The optimal post-workout snack includes both carbs and protein. Together, they work more efficiently. Higher-carb options, such as bagels, fruit, baked potatoes, and cereal, replenish glycogen stores. Add protein (such as yogurt or a protein shake) to help your muscles recover and grow stronger. A smart post-workout snack or drink stops muscle breakdown, rehydrates you, encourages bone repair, and kick-starts adaptations.

If food sounds gross after working out or racing, try drinking a smoothie, chocolate milk, and/or a sports recovery drink immediately, and then eat solid food within a few hours to further boost glycogen. If you're training more than once within eight hours (think: track meet!), it's even more important to refuel right after harder exercise with something both easy and quick to digest, plus some water or a hydrating drink.

Examples

> *Chocolate milk + almonds*
> *Banana + PB + yogurt*
> *Grapes + protein shake*
> *Energy bar with protein*
> *Baked potato + PB or hard-boiled eggs*
> *DIY Smoothie (see recipe, p. 150)*

HYDRATION

You are mostly water. Water keeps everything running smoothly under your skin, including your lungs when you breathe. Your muscles also use water during exercise. When you run, salty water seeps out of your pores as sweat. If you lose enough fluid, you'll become dehydrated, like a raisin; your blood volume decreases, and eventually you'll slow down. All that can definitely affect your performance.

When you lose water and electrolytes (salts and minerals) through sweating, it's important to replenish those fluids so your muscles and body can resume functioning at their best. Factors such as heat, humidity, and training effort definitely affect whether you sweat buckets.

Sip water—the best source!—and other hydrating drinks throughout the day, as well as before, during, and after working out. Stay on top of sipping water especially if you are doing two workouts in a day and if it's hot out. We recommend carrying around a reusable water bottle or stashing one in your locker if drinks aren't allowed in class. Drink to

Sweating it out

What, exactly, is sweat or perspiration? Glitter? Not quite. It's fluid that your two to four million sweat glands release. The fluid, containing salt, is pulled from your bloodstream, through your skin. Sweating is one way your body regulates your temperature; as the water on your skin evaporates, it cools your body.

thirst, and know that hormones can affect your thirst levels and ability to regulate heat. For example, during the second phase of your menstrual cycle, before your period, higher hormones can dampen your natural thirst signal.

The color of your urine is one indicator of hydration. A light golden color is a good sign. If it's dark gold, orange, or brown and concentrated, you're likely dehydrated. If your urine is clear, you might be overhydrated. (Yes, you can be too hydrated. It's called *hyponatremia*, and the symptoms are similar to those of dehydration: nausea, vomiting, headache, confusion, fatigue, irritability, muscle weakness or cramps, seizures, and coma. To avoid this, add fruit juice, electrolytes, coconut water, sports drink, or maple syrup and salt to your water.)

For hot, long, high-hormone, or very active days, try a sports drink with electrolytes (buy one or make your own by adding salt and juice to water). Note that some popular sports drinks are superconcentrated, and others contain artificial sweeteners, both of which might be a little harder for your body to absorb or cause GI distress. Milk or a smoothie after your run are good options too. Practice with different fluids to find what works best for you. Don't forget that some veggies and fruits have high water content as well!

Before vs. after

PRO TIP

Milk is a great choice *after* your workout, but drinking it right *before* practice might upset your stomach. Artificial sweeteners and carbonated drinks (even seltzer), especially before running, can also cause some GI distress.

Examples

- › *Water*
- › *Milk*
- › *Sports drinks*
- › *Fruit juice*
- › *Herbal tea*

- › *Smoothies*
- › *Broths*
- › *Pickle juice*
- › *Melons*
- › *Oranges*

- › *Grapes*
- › *Tomatoes*
- › *Cucumber*
- › *Celery*
- › *Peppers*

SPECIAL DIETS

You might follow a specific diet for religious, cultural, or medical reasons. Or you may be interested in trying a particular diet because it is popular or someone you know is following it. Any restrictive diet should be carefully scrutinized with your health and running in mind. Any time you restrict food groups, you increase physical stress and the chance that certain nutrients—important for good running and a healthy life—could be lacking. Here are a few diets you may be hearing about.

Plant-based diets. It's possible to be a vegetarian or vegan runner and be well fueled, but it requires good planning and diligence. When Melody was a vegetarian, she discovered that hard training left her craving meat along with persistent aches and pains, so she switched back to being a omnivore. She found that she felt better and stronger, and so she knew that this change was working for her. Successful plant-based athletes eat enough of a wide variety of foods and plan ahead, often working with RDs or doctors, to ensure they're getting everything they need from their diet. If you are a vegetarian or vegan, make sure to prioritize energy-dense foods and getting enough protein, iron, B vitamins, and other nutrients that are harder to come by in those diets.

Low-carb/high-fat diets. Paleo, keto, and other low-carb/high-fat diets may be trendy, but they're not helpful for runners—especially young ones. A paleo diet, for example, is very high in fiber—which, in excess, is hard to digest. It also leaves little room for all essential nutrients. No studies have yet shown that keto (which claims to burn fat) will give you any athletic advantage. Carbs, which are nearly MIA from these diets, are crucial for competitive athletes.

Clean eating. The definition of "clean eating" is not clear. Some claim it's an organic, whole-foods-based diet that's full of fruits, veggies, and whole grains and without processed foods. While that approach may boost beneficial antioxidants, vitamins, minerals, and fiber, be wary. For athletes, high bulk and low energy density isn't optimal. The sheer volume and work required to chomp solely on, say, kale, cauliflower, dried beans, and wheat berries displace much-needed energy or nutrients. And the truth is sometimes processed or refined foods can deliver a nutritional punch more efficiently and with less gastric distress. Processed foods are also often cheap and convenient. There's nothing wrong with that.

◊ ◊ ◊

Melody's most heartbreaking race "fail" came at the hands of following a fad diet craze at the time: "food combining." While training sometimes over 100 miles per week for the Olympic Marathon Trials in 2000, she was told not to eat carbs with protein. On the start line of the biggest race of her life, she was glycogen depleted, and at one point, had to crawl on her hands and knees.

In sum, be very cautious when considering fad diets, which can do more harm than good. As you'll hear soon, restricting your food can result in problems and poor health.

When it comes to diets, remember this: Restricting your food stresses your body and mind, which causes cortisol to rise. This affects your pituitary and hormone levels. Restricting food, or obsessing over it, also affects neurotransmitters (the messengers that affect how you think and behave). It also increases anxiety (eek) and decreases serotonin (a feel-good hormone). No thanks.

RECIPES

OVERNIGHT OATS

1 cup water, milk, or kefir
½ cup oats (instant or rolled)*
Dash salt
Dash cinnamon
1 scoop vanilla or chocolate protein powder (whey or plant-based)
Fruit (frozen berries, chopped apple, raisins)
Nuts and seeds (walnuts, chia seeds, coconut, pepitas)
Chocolate chips, if desired

*Or use leftover cooked quinoa or prepared steel-cut oats

Combine all ingredients in a jar, bowl, or sealable container and mix well. Store in the refrigerator overnight or for at least 1–2 hours. Serve cold or hot. Drizzle with yogurt, nut butter, or additional toppings as desired.

VEGETABLE BEEF SOUP

- 2 pounds beef short ribs
- 1 tablespoon olive oil
- 3 quarts water
- 1 large onion, cut into 1-inch pieces
- 2 large cloves garlic, chopped
- 2–3 stalks celery, cut into medium pieces
- ½ head cabbage, coarsely cut
- 3–4 large carrots, cut into medium pieces
- 2 zucchini, cut into chunks
- ¼ pound green beans, cut into halves
- 1 large can whole, peeled tomatoes, cut coarsely, or canned diced tomatoes
- 2 bay leaves
- 1½ teaspoons crushed, dried basil
- Salt and pepper to taste

Optional: kidney beans, corn, peas, barley, rice, or pasta

Lay ribs on a clean surface and dab with paper towels to remove excess moisture. Season lightly with salt and black pepper. In a large soup pot, heat oil on medium heat. When oil is hot, add ribs; brown on each side. Add water. Allow ribs to simmer on medium-high heat for 20 minutes, slightly covered with lid; add water if needed to keep ribs covered. Add the rest* of the ingredients, including spices. Cook until veggies are tender. Add salt and pepper to taste. Note: The longer this soup sits, the better it tastes. Your body will benefit from nutrients in the bones and veggies!

*If adding a grain or pasta, cook separately and add 1 to 1½ cups to soup.

DIY SMOOTHIE

- 1–2   cups liquid (milk, juice, or water)
- 1   banana (or another soft fruit, such as avocado or mango)
- 1   handful frozen or fresh fruit (berries, peaches)
- 1–2   handfuls greens (spinach, kale)
- 2   tablespoons nut butter (peanut butter, sunflower seed butter), seeds (chia), or avocado
- ¼–½   cup rolled oats or instant oatmeal
- 1   scoop protein powder or yogurt (plain or flavored)

Optional add-ins: ginger, cinnamon, shredded coconut, honey, or blackstrap molasses

Place liquid in a blender, followed by solid ingredients. Blend on high until smooth. Add more liquid and stir or scrape with a spatula as needed. Pour into a cup, thermos, or bowl. Sprinkle with optional toppings or additional sliced fruit.

Use this template as a starting point, aiming to include liquid, fruit, veggies, protein, fat, and flavor. Mix and match ingredients from your fridge and pantry until you find your favorite combos of ingredients.

WRITING PROMPTS

Food was central to my family life growing up. Mealtimes were sacred, especially dinner. Food was always associated with togetherness as a family or with friends. —M.F.

What is eating like in your family?

The best meal I ever had (and five things I tasted, smelled, saw, heard, felt)

What makes me feel powerful

9

FOOD & BODY ISSUES

HOW TO TACKLE PROBLEMS HEAD-ON

Something went amiss with eating in middle school. I began to reject the breakfasts my mother lovingly made for me. It's not that the food didn't taste or look appetizing. It's that I was trying to control something, anything. I was using self-denial as a coping mechanism. My mom had cancer, and my dad was an alcoholic who'd lost his job. Plus, I'd tried to fit in with the "in" group of girls at school, but it didn't feel right, so I isolated myself. And I dove head-first into less of everything: less food, less me, less presence.

This landed me in a total fail. By the end of ninth grade, I couldn't finish my favorite race of the year, the Bolder Boulder 10K, let alone repeat as age-group champion. I walked off the course totally discouraged. Hitting my rock bottom hurt. I had let myself down by not eating enough. I'd been hoping to make the varsity cross-country squad in high school that fall and now doubted that I could. But having that goal gave me hope and inspiration to nourish myself. I didn't completely heal my relationship with food until years later. Eating and body issues are complex and require thoughtful treatment. But I'm lucky that my

*love for running, my sky-high goals, and my wanting to be strong for my
mom through her illness guided me away from unhealthy ways of coping, distorted body image, and disordered eating. It took a decade, but
my turnaround started with eating to win in high school.*

*I have a body and soul to feed, and when they're nourished, I have
the power and confidence to help others. And, of course, to race hard.*

—M.F.

As a runner, you might hear comments and judgment about your body
from coaches, parents, teammates, doctors, or Aunt Bertie. Some of what
you hear might be contradictory or make you question yourself. You
might hear criticism about other athletes' bodies too. Often in sport, bodies are weighed, pinched, poked, and prodded. They are criticized, praised,
and dismissed. But just because it's common doesn't mean it's OK.

We authors have enough body-shaming stories to fill another book!
For example, TV commentators referred often to Melody's size (calling
her waif- and nymphlike), and a coach praised Elizabeth for "disappear-
ing before our eyes." Three-time NCAA steeplechase champ (now a pro)
Allie Ostrander was distracted during a championship race by the sta-
dium announcers citing her height and weight multiple times (incor-
rectly, at that). Pro runner Allie Kieffer, after qualifying for the high
school state track meet as a freshman, was told by her science teacher,
"Well, you must have a really big engine in that big of a body." She says
people always told her she'd be better if she lost weight and that she
wasn't built for running.

We live in a world inundated by "diet culture," a system of beliefs that
values certain appearances and behaviors over others. It equates body
appearance, size, and shape with health, approval, and success. It tempts
us with spendy, silly plans promising a better body, faster running, a per-

fect self. With this talk all around you, you might start to wonder whether your worth is in your weight, whether you'd be faster if you were thinner, whether you were built the right way to succeed. You might be tempted by a quick-fix powder or 5 min. abs or a downloadable diet that an influencer posts an #ad for.

That's why we wrote this chapter. Because you deserve the truth: Your appearance and weight do not determine your worth or your success as a runner—no matter what Aunt Bertie says about her low-calorie diet, or what that pro runner posts about what she eats in a day, or what a coach remarks about your changing body. Your body is awesome-amazing-enough, not to mention ever-changing, resilient, and miraculous. It needs fuel, and the fuel you eat will power you to incredible places.

In this chapter, we'll discuss body image and appearance pressures, eating and exercise issues, and the signs that you or someone you know may need to seek help.

THERE IS NO IDEAL RUNNER'S BODY

Have you heard that runners who are thinner are faster? It's a myth, but one that is spread far and wide. We all face pressure about how we look and may struggle at times with expectations and judgments. Sometimes to combat that, among other complex reasons, people try dieting, body-shaming themselves, or overexercising. Those behaviors have long-lasting negative effects. Trying to fit a very specific, unrealistic mold is harmful.

In high school, I was invited twice to run in Japan's world's-qualifying meet, the Chiba International Cross Country event that serves as their national championships. I won both years and set the 4K course record my senior year. Officials hustled me into a tent after that race and asked me to take my shoes off. A man bent down and traced an outline of my feet in order to make custom spikes embroidered with my name. I remember standing there, feeling like a princess, until one of the men looked at me and said, "You gained weight," and spread his arms wide. Immediately, I went from feeling energetic and happy to feeling sad and judged for my body weight. When our bodies are assigned value by how small or big they are, we aren't truly seen. The gift we owe ourselves and each other is to see and honor who we are, not what we look like. —M.F.

Don't let anyone's opinion about how you are "supposed" to look keep you from finding and appreciating your personal strength, power, and endurance. Worrying about and trying to change the way your body looks distracts you from focusing on what you and your body can do! It keeps you from maximizing your potential. It can also lead you to ignore signals your body is sending you that it's time to refuel and recharge. Signals such as hunger and fatigue are not only important clues to your health, they are also good indicators of how your training, racing, and recovery are going. Listen up!

FORGET ABOUT RACING WEIGHT

When people talk about "racing weight," they are referring to a number on the scale that they believe will turn them into the fastest, best runner they can be. That weight is usually a smaller number than they'd nor-

PRO TIP

Any body can be a runner.

mally see when stepping on the scale, which they believe is more efficient for racing.

A weight that guarantees I'll be the fastest runner I can be? Sounds great, right? Nope! Look closer and you will see that "racing weight" is neither accurate nor helpful for runners.

Why? First, weight is arbitrary. The number on the scale is simply a measure of gravity pulling on a body. That number depends on whether you've pooped, how much glycogen you have stored, how much water you've had. Furthermore, it doesn't measure important things, such as your muscle tone or athletic ability.

Second, many circumstances combine to influence the shape a body takes. These factors include genetics, environment, diseases, medication, lifestyle, socioeconomics, and more. Your body does have a set point—a composition it naturally gravitates toward—but even that shifts with time.

Third, some runners try to get to their "racing weight" by cutting back on calories. But restricting calories is neither fun nor productive. It can result in no weight loss or even weight gain. Why? Because the formula "calories in – calories out = weight loss/gain" is wrong. The math just doesn't add up. Metabolism—and oversimplification of a "calorie"—has a lot to do with this.

Basically, your body wants to keep you alive, and when it senses restriction, it holds on to lifesaving energy, such as fat. If an athlete has a history of dieting or weight changes, her metabolism may have already slowed. If an athlete has not restricted before, she might see some weight loss, but initially that loss is water and stored glycogen. (No fun if you're about to race and are dehydrated and weak, an experience Melody had at the 2000 Olympic Marathon Trials.) Regardless of a runner's past dieting history, restricting puts every athlete at risk for the complications of a syndrome called Relative Energy Deficiency in Sport (RED-S), which include bone injuries, hormone disturbances, GI distress, mood effects, and other bummers. (More on that later in this chapter.)

Fourth, losing weight can mean losing strength—a disadvantage on the course, track, road, and trail. Research suggests that achieving an idealized weight or body composition through severe and persistent energy restriction will negatively affect your performance and health. Who wants that?

Finally, how you perform on race day is the product of countless details. Think of it like making pancakes, a simple dish yet one that turns out differently depending on the recipe, ingredients, heat, cooking oil, pan, and how good a flipper you are. In training, your body and mind are altered by the process and ingredients too. Running, recovery, and strength training alter your body and mind—as do nutrition, hydration, and hormones. On race day, many external factors can affect results,

---

 My teammate went on a diet—maybe even has an eating disorder—and she got faster. Will that work for me?

Some runners who try to get down to "racing weight" or fit a running-specific thin ideal by restricting food or losing weight might see an initial increase in performance, and they might even say they feel "great." *But this is temporary.* Stress hormones mask fatigue. The athlete may get feelings of euphoria (a symptom associated with starving), a short-term increase in oxygen uptake, the sensation of feeling lighter, and maybe even praise from others. But subsequent decline includes injury, fatigue, binge-and-purge cycles, and loss of euphoria, among other health issues. Every body is different, so it's hard to predict when negative consequences will hit. But they will. And the earlier the intervention, the better the outcome. Avoid dieting. And if you're concerned about someone, see p. 170.

such as weather, strategy, mental prep, confidence, fatigue, and stress. "Racing weight," then, is neither the cause nor guarantee of success.

You might look around at a race or on your Insta feed and see a bunch of lean runners. Remember: Appearance doesn't determine success, and weight is merely one of infinite details that may influence performance. Trying to look a certain way (like a teammate or celebrity or track pro you admire) is a harmful trap. If you are training appropriately for your goal, fueling, sleeping, and taking care of yourself, and are otherwise healthy, then your body will take the shape and weight that is right for you. That's the vessel in which you will run at your best. It flows naturally from working *with* your body, not against it.

RUNNING ON EMPTY: THE DANGERS OF UNDERFUELING

It's not only people on diets or with eating disorders who face the pitfalls of not eating enough. Some runners underfuel accidentally. Not eating enough can happen for several reasons: a busy schedule, a lack of nutrition education (not knowing the importance of things such as consistent fueling and post-workout snacks), increasing training load without upping daily intake, food insecurity, or not planning—for example, forgetting to pack a snack or lunch. Plus, as a busy, growing athlete, it's easy to underestimate your nutrition needs. No matter the reason, insufficient nutrition affects your body. In this section, we'll talk about how underfueling compromises both your running and overall well-being.

Chronic low energy availability (LEA) occurs when energy taken in from food and drink isn't enough to fuel daily functions and growth, plus daily activities and exercise. Remember the nutrition balance seesaw (p. 132)? When your energy seesaw is chronically off-kilter, without enough energy to support you and your activities, that's called LEA.

WHAT'S ᴛʜᴇ DEAL ᴡɪᴛʜ RED-S

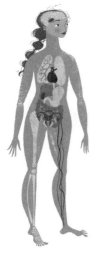

Blood

Growth & development

Pyschology

Cardiovascular system

Gastrointestinal system

Immunity

Menstrual function

Bones

Endocrine system

Metabolism

HEALTH

Decreased concentration

Irritability

Depression

Decreased glycogen stores

Decreased muscle strength

Decreased endurance performance

Increased injury risk

Decreased training adaptations/response

Impaired judgment

Decreased coordination

PERFORMANCE

The symptoms and consequences of Relative Energy Deficiency in Sport (RED-S), which is caused by low energy availability (LEA).

In time, that imbalance can cause problems in your body, from your heart and brain to your bones and blood. The effects are complex and intertwined, but scientists and doctors have started connecting the dots. They've named the resulting web of complications Relative Energy Deficiency in Sport (RED-S)—a syndrome that hinders both health and performance. It is caused by LEA. Any athlete who doesn't get enough nutrition risks RED-S. Researchers continue to uncover more details about RED-S, including that it affects all athletes—not just females—but includes the female athlete triad (energy, period, and bone issues, previously recognized in female athletes).

Let's look closer at what LEA and RED-S entail and their symptoms.

CONSEQUENCES OF LEA AND RED-S

Without adequate fuel, your body begins to cancel nonvital functions (digestion, metabolism, and preparing for pregnancy, to name a few) in order to save energy for vital functions (your heart beating and lungs breathing, for example). In sum, your body does the best it can to help you survive.

Here are key areas in your body that are affected by LEA and RED-S.

Endocrine system. Remember hormones, those chemical messengers we talked about in Chapter 2? They're integral to your endocrine system, which also includes glands, such as the pituitary and thyroid. LEA interrupts your hormones' work, including the important feedback loop between your hypothalamus, pituitary, and ovaries, which controls your period. LEA disrupts other hormones too, including those that influence your appetite, blood sugar, cell growth and repair, and stress levels. Hormones are important for adapting to training, so jeopardizing them jeopardizes all the hard work you put into running.

Skeleton. LEA can hurt your bones. One measure of bone health is bone mineral density (BMD), and LEA decreases it. As humans, we have a limited window to build up bone strength for life, and low estrogen (a symptom of LEA) hinders bone formation, which decreases bone strength and puts you at risk for bone stress injuries. Stress reactions and fractures—the overuse injuries to bones common in runners—are no fun.

Heart. LEA affects your ticker by creating dysfunction, less-than-ideal blood lipids (think: cholesterol), and compromised blood pressure. That's dangerous.

Metabolism. LEA has been shown to reduce resting metabolic rate (RMR), which is basically how much energy your body uses when you are at rest, for example, lying on the couch watching movies. A decreasing RMR affects your body composition by potentially increasing body fat and decreasing muscle.

Iron levels. LEA and iron levels are linked. Iron, the mineral essential for using oxygen, plays an important role in your blood health. Being deficient in iron or iron stores (ferritin) decreases your appetite, among other issues, which may contribute to LEA.

Growth. Research on athletes who had severe energy imbalances showed disruptions in growth hormone, which is essential for healthy development as well as adaptations to training.

Digestive system. Effects of LEA on your digestive system go beyond "runner's trots." Severe LEA has been shown to mess with the sphincter, constipation, and stool leakage. Yuck.

Immunity. Studies suggest that your immunity (your ability to fight off sickness) is compromised with LEA. Athletes with inadequate intake have higher risks of illness, including respiratory and GI issues.

Mood and well-being. There's a two-way street between LEA and your psychological health. Research has found that athletes who don't get enough fuel also have less ability to deal with stress and negative moods.

None of those consequences are beneficial to you as a human, let alone as a runner who's looking to excel in sport. Speaking of performing at your best in your sport, LEA and RED-S will certainly negatively affect that too. Here's how research shows chronic low energy can play out for athletes:

› Increases injury risk
› Decreases endurance performance
› Decreases muscle strength
› Decreases glycogen stores
› Decreases training response
› Impairs judgment
› Decreases coordination
› Decreases concentration and cognition
› Increases irritability
› Increases depression

Clearly, restricting food and undereating sets you back over the long haul. It happened to us and to other runners, but it doesn't have to happen to you. Imagine the amazing heights to which you can take yourself, your teammates, and your sport without such hang-ups! The sky is your limit.

You can't tell someone is experiencing LEA or RED-S by just looking at them. And LEA and RED-S are not only found in people with eating disorders. In fact, according to experts, many young runners experience LEA, and potentially RED-S, involuntarily. As we mentioned, this can happen without you even realizing it! Perhaps it's due to busyness, stress, an increase in training without an increase in fueling, or other factors.

So how, exactly, do you know if you have a problem? In theory, coaches are in a good position to identify athletes with LEA and RED-S, but some might not understand the complexities or notice that something's off. But if *you* know and feel that something is off or you are exhibiting symptoms, it's important to seek help. Doctors, registered dietitians (RDs), and psychologists or psychiatrists can be helpful. They should be familiar with LEA, RED-S, sports medicine and nutrition, endocrinology, and/or eating disorders. Seeing a specialist, such as a sports endocrinologist or metabolic bone expert, especially one who's well-versed in young athletes, is also a smart choice. (See Chapter 10.)

Identifying these issues can be complicated. It's a diagnosis of exclusion, meaning your doctor will need to cross other potential issues off her list before determining whether you're dealing with RED-S. A doctor will want to rule out, say, an infection or endocrine disorders. Screening tools exist to pinpoint RED-S, but they are in their infancy—and some docs aren't yet aware of them. Another hard thing about diagnosing RED-S and LEA is that it is challenging to accurately measure energy intake and output.

The energy required for your body to maintain a period—and other signs of health—differs from your teammates'. Every athlete has her own seesaw to balance. That's why you need to look at the signs you get from your body. Signs of LEA could include irregular or absent periods, repeated illness, persistent or frequent injury, or mood changes. A clinician might test hormonal levels, ask about your fueling, and look for additional and related factors that hurt performance, such as iron deficiency.

Figuring out if you are experiencing LEA, RED-S, or another issue doesn't have to take thousands of dollars of testing. Simply asking the question is an invitation for you to fuel consistently and sufficiently, respect and listen to what your body is telling you, and speak up when you need help or feel confused. If you are experiencing RED-S, treatment may involve changing some of your exercise and nutrition habits. This could include upping your intake, tweaking your food choices, timing your fuel more efficiently, prioritizing certain nutrients, and recognizing ebbs and flows in your fueling needs (RDs are pros at this). It also may include increasing your rest and recovery, and maybe reducing or stopping exercise. Cognitive behavioral therapy (CBT), among other approaches, has also shown promise in this area (see p. 96).

Moderating or returning to training and competition should be a group effort. It's important that everyone on your support team communicates with one another. That means you, your parents, and the specialists you're working with should communicate with your coaches and athletic trainers. They need to be on the same page to help you stay healthy and run strong.

DISORDERED EATING AND EATING DISORDERS

At least 30 million Americans have had an eating disorder (ED). Of all mental health disorders, EDs have the second highest mortality rate, which means people die as a result. And they're not limited to lean, skinny, fast, white, or female runners; everyone faces cultural pressures around appearance and eating and is therefore susceptible to food and body issues.

EDs, which include specific diagnoses such as anorexia and bulimia, sit on one end of the food-and-body-issue spectrum. Disordered eating (DE) sits at the other end, but shares signs with EDs and has serious implications as well. This continuum is full of blurry lines and overlapping symptoms, so know that you or your teammates don't have to fit into a specific square box to struggle with these issues.

Let's start with a closer look at disordered eating. DE involves irregular eating behaviors and nutrition habits and may include frequent dieting or restricting; food-related anxiety; skipping meals; chronic weight changes; rigid rules or rituals around food and exercise; or feeling guilt and shame with eating or a preoccupation with food, weight, or body image.

Up to 40 percent of adolescent female athletes in aesthetic sports, such as gymnastics, where appearance is judged as key to performance, show signs of disordered eating, and more than 40 percent of Division I and III athletes met criteria for disordered eating. Eighty-four percent of NCAA athletes show maladaptive eating behaviors. Consequences are serious, including injury, bone loss, GI issues, dehydration, heart issues, and increased anxiety, depression, and isolation. Research has shown that high school female athletes who reported disordered eating were twice as likely to suffer from a muscle or bone injury. Poor fueling leads to poor performance, plus a host of health problems with RED-S.

Disordered eating can also lead to eating disorders, life-threatening illnesses that include severe disturbances in behaviors, emotions, and body image, including a preoccupation with food and weight. Many folks with EDs have another mental health issue they are dealing with, such as anxiety, panic, or obsessive-compulsive disorder. Eating disorders have a high mortality rate and require treatment.

Here's a brief look at the most common EDs.

Anorexia nervosa. Limiting food intake, fear of being "fat," often compulsive exercise; especially damaging to heart, muscles, bones, skin, and hair. Young people with this disorder have 10 times the risk of dying compared to their peers.

Bulimia nervosa. Binge-eating, purging by vomiting or laxatives; especially damaging to throat, neck glands, face, teeth, digestion, intestines, and kidneys.

Binge-eating disorder. Binge-eating, feeling out of control; can lead to diabetes, hypertension, and cardiovascular disease. This disorder is at least three times more common than anorexia and bulimia combined.

Orthorexia. Obsession with "healthy" or "clean" eating, compulsive checking of ingredients and nutritional information, restricting food groups, extreme interest in "safe," "healthy," or "pure" foods. Consequences include nutritional deficiencies, digestive complications, and other risks.

Fork the Food Police!

* Thinner, lighter, and/or leaner does not equal faster.

* You do not have to "earn" food.

* Exercise is not punishment for eating.

* There is no single or perfect runner diet.

* You have permission to eat what you want.

* What you see on social media isn't the whole picture.

COMPULSIVE EXERCISE

Sometimes called exercise addiction, compulsive exercise is when you exercise too much, with harmful consequences. Someone with this condition might exercise persistently and excessively, not because she enjoys it, but rather because she feels like she *must* do so in order to avoid a negative consequence. It's common for people to use exercise as a way of coping with stress and emotions. But while running may feel therapeutic, it's no cure for mental health issues, such as anxiety and depression, and is certainly not a substitute for therapy, medication, or other treatment.

Signs of this condition include exercising to avoid feeling guilty or working out in secret. Exercise becomes compulsive when it interferes with important activities in your life or you continue to do it despite injury or medical issues. Someone with an exercise compulsion might feel anxious, depressed, irritable, or distressed when they do not exercise. Some consequences of exercise addiction include persistent soreness and pain, injuries, fatigue, reduced immunity, bone loss, and hormonal issues.

WHERE TO FIND HELP

Do any of the symptoms or signs outlined above sound familiar? Help is a click, text, or call away. Beating eating and body issues requires intervention and assistance from trained medical professionals. Recovery is possible. You are worth it. The sooner you intervene in these diseases, habits, and behaviors, the better the potential outcome.

Ideally, treatment is comprehensive, including expert medical, psychological, and nutritional care, and addresses both emotional and physical symptoms. Treatment teams should work closely with you, and also with your parents, coaches, and athletic trainers. A team approach accelerates and facilitates recovery. See Chapter 10 for recommended professionals and their qualifications, but whomever you see should be willing and able to refer you to specialists as needed.

There are different kinds of treatment—in-hospital, outpatient, residential (aka you stay somewhere), remote or telemedicine help, weekly therapy sessions, and in-person support groups. Free resources are available too and can also be effective.

How to Talk to a Friend Who Might Be Struggling with Food, Body, or Exercise Issues

Do:

* Choose a good time and place for personal conversations (such as when you're alone, not on a group run).

* Ask: How are you?

* Use "I" statements. ("I am concerned because you haven't been keeping up. Are you feeling OK?")

* Focus on facts. ("I've seen you at the gym for hours at a time.")

* Offer to help and listen. ("I'm here for you, no matter what.")

* Remove stigma. ("I am your friend and won't judge you for anything you tell me.")

* Share your own struggles, if you have them, with DE or ED, compulsive exercise, or body dissatisfaction.

* Stay calm and be supportive.

* Share and reach out to:

    The National Eating Disorders Association (NEDA)
    Toll-free, confidential helpline 1-800-931-2237
    http://myneda.org/helpline-chat
    24/7 crisis support via text (send NEDA to 741-741)

Do not:

* Make promises that you won't or shouldn't keep.

* Comment on weight or appearance.

* Engage in fat-talk or body-shaming.

* Pretend you're not concerned if you are.

* Take their anger, defensiveness, or denial personally.

* Try to treat your friend yourself (rather, do refer them to NEDA's website or a trusted adult, such as a coach, athletic trainer, or parent).

* Give nutritional advice.

WRITING PROMPTS

What messages about bodies do I hear in my daily life?

When someone comments about how I look

What is one positive change I can make today toward pursuing a healthy athlete ideal?

My body is my friend, and it gives me

10

BUILDING A GREAT TEAM

IT TAKES A VILLAGE, AND
THESE ARE THE PEOPLE YOU WANT IN IT

Some people think running is an individual sport. And it's true that the most important person when it comes to your running is, well, you. For sure, you're your own most valuable resource—something we'll discuss in this chapter.

But there's more to it than that.

Ask any elite or lifelong runner about their running journey and they'll likely tell you about their behind-the-scenes team—coaches, parents, doctors, massage therapists, teammates, and other support crew members who've helped them keep running strong. Running can be an incredible team effort. The team that rallies around you is integral to you running strong.

Building strong teams starts with you developing your own sense of self and intuition and learning how to filter what's important and what's not (called discernment). Along your journey, you'll need to figure out who's on your team, which involves asking questions and the occasional tough conversation. Finally, you need to know whom to ask and how to ask for help when you need it.

All this can be tricky and feel like a heavy responsibility. But you can handle it. We see you. You're strong, capable, conscientious, and smart. Our goal in this chapter is to arm you with useful tools—such as learning to trust your gut, separating fact from fiction, and asking important questions—so you can navigate your own running journey, build an awesome team, and maximize your potential!

INTUITION: TRUST YOUR GUT

Running helps us figure out who we are. It hones your sense of self because it asks you to pay attention to what's happening in and around your body and mind. The more you practice paying attention, the more you'll develop your intuition—the ability to trust your gut. This means listening to the little voice that whispers to you from somewhere inside, respecting the fire in your belly!

To learn to tune in to your intuition, notice the sensations you feel in your body when someone is speaking to you or when you are walking alone and notice something. Do you feel anything in your gut or heart? Does it feel like an expansion or more like a contraction? Generally, the former is positive, saying, "Tell me more!" and the latter is negative and asks, "Wait, what's this?"

Developing this spidey sense takes time, practice, and—you guessed it—respecting the signs your body sends. (See Chapter 6 for a deeper discussion and more practical tips on how to do this.)

DISCERNMENT: PICK YOUR FILTERS WISELY

You've got lots of info coming at you, from feeds, vloggers, coaches, friends, even this book, all churning out content and seeking to get your attention. The key to figuring out what to listen to amid all that noise? Discernment—which means filtering information and then deciding

Truth or fiction?

On screens, in print, and online, you'll find boatloads of information. Some of it is well researched and true, such as fact-checked articles written by ethical journalists and peer-reviewed journal articles; some of it is misguided or incorrect, aka actual fake news. Unfortunately, lies can be catchy and spread quickly. One example of misinformation that is harmful to runner girls is the idea that puberty is a curse—a myth someone maybe heard from someone in a position of power (like a coach) and shared. Misinformation like this isn't backed up by facts or hard data, and it's unhelpful because it may send you down a dangerous path. When you read or hear something that seems questionable, ask yourself: Who's sharing this? Why? Where's the evidence? Is it verifiable?

whether or how it matters to you. Discernment means taking a second to question what someone is telling you and why, and whether it seems legit. Just because an adult says it or you see it online doesn't necessarily make it true.

Practicing discernment also means deciding whether that info aligns with (or challenges) your core values. Once you've figured that out, you can use it, shelve it, or toss it. The point is to take the time to question what's what.

Practicing discernment is another skill that takes practice. The point? Keep trying, learning, listening. That's how you get to know yourself and decipher what's best for you.

What if my coach doesn't listen to me? Or scares me, and I don't know how to bring up an issue?

Ideally, everyone in your running community supports your best interests by listening, making time for you, and taking what you say seriously. In reality, that's not always the case. Navigating some relationships can be tricky. There's a fine line between trust and obedience, between having loyalty and a healthy two-way relationship, between qualifications and merit, especially when one party has power over you (usually the adult). Is there someone else you trust or respect whom you could talk to about your issue? An athletic trainer, assistant coach, parent, or captain? The key is speaking up to someone who will listen to and advocate for—and with—you.

ISO A SUPPORT CREW: ROLE MODELS

Role models—people you admire and who inspire you—are important pillars in running communities. Melody had many positive role models, including her marathoning middle school guidance counselor and her PE teacher and track coach, a former NFL player who told her, "Take it in stride, Melody, take it in stride." His advice was especially helpful when mean middle school boys made fun of her (probably because they couldn't keep up during the schoolwide mile run).

One of her favorite coaches, Beth Alford-Sullivan, spoke with her often about her goals and dreams. "I was inspired to be the best version of myself possible while working with her," says Melody. "I trusted her; there was never any reason for me to think of doing anything other than what she suggested. I knew she believed in me and in my dreams."

For pro Allie Kieffer, one role model in particular stands out. "My mom has been the voice inside that's just been telling me that I can, that I am enough, that I will win, that I can achieve anything that I set myself up for, that I just have to work hard, and I can beat anything," she says.

That's the power of a positive role model. What supporters play big roles in your life? Older teammates, parents, guardians, teachers, coaches? Do you fear or respect them?

My parents were very independent—not mainstream. My sisters and I were encouraged to question everything. I listened respectfully to my high school coach but would get bored with repetitive details. Later, as a pro, one of my coaches asked for total trust, and I complied—even when my gut told me it wasn't best for me. In that instance, it was hard to exercise discernment, and it became a painful lesson that damaged my ability to trust. —M.F.

DEALING WITH DRAMA AND DISTRACTIONS

Growing up isn't just about your developing body; it includes your mental and social development too. This may come with some upheaval that affects both your life and your running, especially as you begin to explore and define your own beliefs, goals, and values. In our busy, complicated, messy world, this phase can be dizzying and uncomfortable and awesome.

Some girls explore risky behaviors and test boundaries (driving, trying new sports, going to unsupervised parties, doing drugs, drinking). While illegal or life-threatening activities should definitely not be on your to-do list, know that new experiences help you develop your identity and independence. Meaningful rites of passage often contain an element of risk that challenges both your discernment and your grit.

Another complication? Screens. As adolescents become increasingly digitally connected, it—ironically—can lead to isolation. How much time do you spend in front of screens—phones, computers, TVs? (On average, American tweens and teens spend six to nine hours a day on games and social media. Yikes!)

Most teens have a smartphone. (We do, too.) It seems like everyone is attached around the clock. Smartphones and their apps offer endless distractions, and it's all too easy to compare yourself to the images and info you're being bombarded with, especially if you're looking at idealized bodies and filtered images on social media. It can make us feel like something is missing, wrong, or less than enough in our own lives. RD Megan Medrano points out that running-specific content often promotes an unhealthy diet culture: body stereotypes, a drive for thinness, eating and workout recommendations that may be ill-advised or not suited to you, revealing uniforms, and more. Does this narrow view help you? Not so much!

What's worse, research shows that most girls see body-shaming and negative messages on social media at least once a week. More than half of teens have been bullied or harassed online. Even posting selfies may increase anxiety and decrease confidence. As few as 30 minutes a day can change the way we view our bodies, make us susceptible to cruel trolls, and more susceptible to loneliness and depression.

Phones do more than pull us into unnecessary drama: they disrupt our sleep and interfere with IRL relationships. We don't mean to gloss over inspirational, motivating, or informative content—it's out there,

Speak Up and Reach Out

If you are being harassed, threatened, or bullied, online or in real life, in particular by an adult, tell someone—a counselor, teacher, sports psychologist, anyone you trust. Know you can always email us (girlsrunningbook@gmail.com); we promise to take you seriously because that's what you deserve.

No More FOMO

What can we do to create space for ourselves, teammates, and friends beyond screens?

With your team, can you make a pact to do any of the following?

* DND settings on at 9:00 p.m.
* Turn off notifications on social media apps.
* Keep your phone in your backpack at practice so you can talk to your teammates during warm-ups and easy runs without distractions.
* Host an unfollow party: Clean up your feeds by unfollowing accounts that make you feel less than enough. Seek out a diverse range of accounts to follow beyond running (body positive folx, animals, nature photographers, musicians, artists, etc.).
* Skip Strava for metrics/run data (GPS is wildly unreliable and wonky, anyway), or set a time limit.
* Take a one-week, or even a one-day, detox from social media.

especially coming from young people like you! For example, pro Allie Ostrander used social media to speak truth to race announcers who were fixated on her appearance during the NCAA championships. It's also a great way to connect with running and other communities. We wish all social media was productive like this—focused on body positivity, inclusivity, and community.

As someone who always speaks up online, pro runner Allie Kieffer receives a lot of feedback (good, bad, and ugly). Being constantly scrutinized isn't always fun, she admits, but for every one bad message she receives, she cherishes two good ones and reminds herself that it is the trolls who are insecure. What's more, she unfollows anyone who doesn't make her feel good and limits her time on social. "I don't want to get bogged down with things that make me feel bad about myself," she says. Work to build your own impenetrable armor so haters' words bounce off.

ISO A SUPPORT CREW: WHOM TO TALK TO ABOUT WHAT, PLUS QUESTIONS TO ASK THEM

One reason runners need to build a team is because neither you nor any one crew member is an expert in everything. That's where people with different specialties come in.

Finding the right crew is like piecing a puzzle together. And it can take a few tries. For example, when you need to call in expert advice, you might need to navigate complicated systems, like the health care industry. And sometimes medical providers aren't familiar with athletes' health concerns. One way to find out is to look for signs that they have an interest or knowledge in sports. Try checking out their "About me" page for athlete-focused research, credentials with a sports-specific focus, or even a mention that they run marathons.

Two important questions to ask any specialist are about their approach and process: What is their philosophy and background? What are the steps to working with them? Ideally, the specialist's answers demonstrate that they will be a helpful member of your support crew. Everyone on your team should do their best to address your issues or, if need be, refer you to someone who can.

Let's take a closer look at some of the people you may want on your team, the qualifications to look for, and the questions you might need to ask them to advocate for your best runner self.

COACHES

Coaches are in charge of training, competition, and most aspects of your cross country, track and field, and other teams. They can be inspirational, motivational, educational, and great role models. The best coaches do it because they love the sport, the camaraderie, and helping athletes reach their potential.

Qualifications. There's no official standard for being a running coach. There are a handful of certifications, including through USA Track & Field, the nationwide governing body, with basic sport-specific education. A coach's primary goal should be to keep an athlete healthy and injury-free. Other coaching priorities should include helping athletes prevent burnout and honoring each runner as a person, not just a number. They should keep an athlete's long-term development in mind with a big-picture approach to training and competition and foster a positive team culture. When it comes to health and safety, they should be certified in first aid, CPR, and concussion protocols, and prioritize mental health. Plus, we recommend coaches register with the US Center for SafeSport, an organization that aims to prevent emotional, physical, and

---

PRO TIP

Private coaches

Some athletes hire private coaches who aren't affiliated with their schools for mentorship, extra guidance, or year-round training and competition. Depending on the season and situation, this can be fruitful or cause tension with your school coach and team. Communicate honestly with your school coach, including your dreams and goals, and give them a chance to help you thrive. Consider what you can do to help your team thrive, too. Even world-class teen runners find perks of committing to their school teams, including taking on leadership responsibilities. A sense of service to that which is greater than ourselves empowers and energizes us.

sexual abuse of athletes and includes training on creating safe environments for athletes.

Q's

> Can you explain this workout so I can better understand why I'm doing it?
> Are you familiar with LEA, RED-S, or the female athlete triad and their consequences? How do you address those issues? Where do you refer athletes with those issues?

Q's for your school or sport organization about coaches, according to the US Center for SafeSport

> Are staff subject to background checks?
> What training do you provide or require for coaches, managers, trainers, and volunteers to protect the well-being of athletes?
> What policies and best practices do you employ to protect athletes, and how do you enforce them?
> If there is a concern, where do I report an issue?

REGISTERED DIETITIANS (RD)

These fueling and hydration experts are very helpful for any athlete, especially athletes who want to optimize their nutrition and maintain an appropriate energy balance, as well as those who are struggling with disordered eating.

Qualifications. Although anyone can call themselves a "nutritionist," only those with an RD have six-plus years of education plus pass a credentialing test and extensive internship. An RD is a much better source than fitness trackers and calorie counters, cookbooks and vlogs, social

CLOSER LOOK

Hey, Coach!

Many coaches have your best interest in mind. Some don't. If a coach says unhelpful or disrespectful things that make you feel diminished, especially when it comes to appearance, weight, and expectations, you should speak up, if not to the coach directly, then to another trusted adult. If it is easier to write a letter or email, here are thoughts you might share with a coach or athletic director, aimed at creating a positive team environment.

Coach, please don't . . .

* Comment on my weight, shape, or appearance
* Weigh athletes, post body-composition numbers, or set parameters around those metrics
* Engage in diet talk (calories, diets, "earning" food, etc.)
* Equate thinness, appearance, or performance with fastness or OK-ness
* Ignore me if I'm not the fastest
* Gauge success only by wins and losses

Coach, please do . . .

* Explain what you expect from us
* Prioritize rest and recovery
* Create a safe, supportive environment
* Ask me how I'm doing—mentally, physically, socially
* Defer and refer to medical professionals when it comes to nutrition, mental health, and other health issues
* Guide me toward improvement as an athlete and a person
* Share your love of running as a lifelong pursuit

media and blogs, which give only a small snapshot that's not likely accurate for adolescent runner girls.

Look for an RD who is licensed, with specialization or certification in sports or eating disorders. They should have an antidiet, Intuitive Eating, and/or Health at Every Size approach.

Q's

> Do you work with female runners?
> How do you screen for and help runners address LEA, RED-S, and the female athlete triad and their consequences?
> Can you help me tune in to my body's hunger cues?

ATHLETIC TRAINERS

They can be your first line of defense against injuries and other sidelining issues. We're not talking about a personal trainer, say, at a local gym, but someone employed by your school or team to prioritize athlete well-being.

Qualifications. Athletic trainers must have an athletic training degree and be nationally certified. Most states require licenses too. Some trainers have additional training in running gait and injuries. Jesseca Holcomb, head athletic trainer at Rhodes College, says athletic trainers should take a comprehensive approach that considers your unique training, recovery, and background. "Don't listen to an athletic trainer that tells you just to stretch and ice or that just treats the site of pain. Most chronic injuries take patience and a plan," she says.

Q's

> How can you help me prevent injuries?
> Are you familiar with LEA, RED-S, and the female athlete triad and their consequences? How do you screen for and treat them, and to whom do you refer athletes with those issues?
> What are your expectations of me when it comes to communication or daily routines?
> When are you available—before, after, or during practice and meets?

MENTAL HEALTH PRACTITIONERS

These experts can help in so many ways! Including counselors and therapists, they're essential team players who help you tackle issues such as stress, depression, anxiety, and sports performance, plus provide perspective and foster resilience.

Qualifications. There are stringent standards for a range of mental health practitioners, who have differing scopes and skills. Ask your school counselor, pediatrician, or coach for a referral, says Dr. Marilou Shaughnessy. "Sometimes you don't find the right match the first time," she cautions. You know it's a good fit if they're collaborative and open to questions.

> **Psychologists.** These practitioners, who have a PhD in clinical psychology or counseling or similar, evaluate and provide therapy. Some have training to provide cognitive behavioral therapy or dialectical behavior therapy (both of which are helpful for treating disordered eating and eating disorders, and for providing sports-specific therapy).

> **Psychiatrists.** Psychiatrists are licensed medical doctors who diagnose conditions, prescribe and monitor medications, and provide therapy.

> **Counselors and therapists.** Licensed clinicians should have a master's degree. They evaluate mental health and use a range of therapeutic techniques.

> **Pastoral counselors.** These are clergy members with training in counseling.

> **Social workers.** Whether they're providing case management or a resource, they should have a master's or bachelor's degree along with a license or certification.

Q's

> What is your philosophy and training? Do you incorporate mindfulness or other intuitive practices?
> Do you practice CBT?
> Do you work with female athletes, and if so, what issues do you commonly treat or assist in the care of?
> Are you familiar with or specialized in dealing with disordered eating or other mental health issues that athletes face?

PHYSICAL THERAPISTS (PT)

PTs are your go-to for persistent or nagging injuries. They can empower you with specific strengthening work, manual therapy, and a plan of action to return to running—or keep you running strong.

Qualifications. Physical therapists have a doctoral or postgraduate professional degree and must be licensed by their state. Some specialize in running gait assessment; hands-on treatments, such as soft tissue mobilization; or even pelvic floor therapy. No matter who you see, you should get a game plan with action items that are tailored to getting you back to the demands of your sport, says Dr. Ellie Somers, physical therapist and running coach.

Q's

> Do you work with female athletes and runners?
> What is your approach to treating runners?
> How frequently and long do patients see you for running injuries?
> Do you screen for LEA, RED-S, and the female athlete triad and their consequences? Where do you refer athletes with those issues?

MASSAGE THERAPISTS, CHIROPRACTORS, ACUPUNCTURISTS

These body-work pros can be helpful, depending on what you need. Their fields have narrower scopes of expertise than PTs.

Qualifications. Any practitioner should be licensed and experienced in working with runners. Massage therapists, for example, should be licensed by the state and, in some cases, the city they work in. Look for "LMT" credentials and years of experience, and take recommendations from a trusted doctor, physical therapist, coach, or teammate.

Q's

> Do you work with female athletes and runners?
> What techniques do you use?
> How frequently and long do clients see you for running injuries?
> Are you aware of LEA, RED-S, and the female athlete triad and their consequences? Where do you refer athletes with those issues?

MEDICAL DOCTORS (MD)

These medical experts include those with wide-ranging specialties who can help diagnose and treat injuries and illness and also prescribe medications with a keen eye for your overall health.

Young athletes should see a physician at least once a year for their physical exam required to play sports. A solid family doctor or ob-gyn will understand the menstrual cycle as an indicator of your overall health and will look beyond simply, say, prescribing birth control pills to "treat" missing or otherwise irregular periods.

Qualifications. All doctors should be licensed and board-certified. Look for specialties, such as pediatricians (until you're 18 years old), sports medicine, endocrinology (hormones, bones), and ob-gyn (reproductive issues).

Health care practitioners

PRO TIP

Other medical professionals may be helpful too, including physician assistants (PAs) and nurse practitioners (NPs). Note that naturopaths (NDs), who practice alternative medicine, may recommend herbs, which can be as potent as medicine, but are not regulated or monitored for safety, quality, or dosing—proceed with caution especially if you don't want to fail a drug test!

Q's

> Do you treat female athletes, and are you familiar with the unique stressors of runners?
> Do you treat disordered eating and eating disorders or refer patients elsewhere for those conditions?
> Are you familiar with LEA, RED-S, and the female athlete triad and their consequences? How do you screen for or treat them?
> Are you willing to test ferritin (iron stores), bone density, or other labs specific to female athletes?

STRENGTH COACHES

A strength coach can be a useful resource for developing your neuromuscular prowess and power.

Qualifications. Seek out someone experienced at training athletes who has appropriate certifications. A good strength coach will teach you how to perform strength movements correctly, not just give you a tough workout.

Q's

> Do you work with female athletes and runners?
> Can you help me with training proper movement mechanics and technique?

CAPTAINS

Your team leaders should be role models and can be wonderful allies and resources for you.

Qualifications. Either voted by team or appointed by coach, someone who steps up and takes on an important leadership role.

Q's
> Can you support me when I need to tell Coach something and am scared to do it?
> How can I help you? The team?

BACK TO YOU: BEING A TEAMMATE

One of the best things about running is that it introduces you to amazing people. Our teammates became our best friends, bridesmaids, and go-to rocks. We've shared deep conversations, belly laughs, and countless secrets. They give us courage and lift our hearts. Teammates who become friends make running (and life) so much richer. When we invest in each other, it helps everyone become her best self.

What does it take to be an awesome teammate? Melody always appreciated helpful, honest, cheerful teammates, especially those who shared feedback and support openly. Dr. Nicole Hagobian, a sports psychology consultant and professor, recommends aiming to be the kind of teammate that you yourself would like to have. "The more each athlete takes responsibility for her own actions and behaviors and takes pride in being a member of her team by showing up to practice on time, ready to go, with a positive attitude, the more her teammates will emulate this," she says. Do you show up every day, participate in meets, and support your team? How do you support and help others improve or reach their goals?

Remember, cross country and track and field are team sports. "Although running is considered a 'coactive' sport, meaning athletes perform side-by-side versus directly together, runners still benefit greatly from a high level of team cohesion," Hagobian says.

Research supports that idea too. Studies have shown that everyone performs better when they feel connected to their team, especially women. Having an "every athlete for herself" mentality isn't very useful, or much fun. When we look beyond ourselves and aim to be a positive, contributing member of a team, we actually help ourselves perform better. "Serving others is actually self-serving as well in the end, so everyone wins," says Hagobian.

Building a great team means building connections and quality relationships within that team. What can you do to contribute to that? Here are five ideas for strengthening your team:

Create team goals. Uniting around running-related tasks and dreams can bring your team together. Sit down together for a goal-setting session at the beginning of the season. How will each athlete contribute as an individual to the team goal?

Foster team culture. What daily actions can you take to create a positive environment? Ideas include supporting each other during workouts, cheering for every runner at races, taking easy days easy, and avoiding one-stepping. Consider planning team events or meet-ups to just hang out together, building stronger bonds off the track.

Share an identity. Can you find something that physically unites the team beyond uniforms? What about bright socks, a unique prerace cheer, or a special high-five rally at the finish line? Create your own traditions. This support and care will bolster your identity and strength as a team.

Deal with toxicity. Sometimes you get stuck on a team or with a teammate who makes you feel lousy. First, know that the people creating drama are often struggling with something themselves. Second, is there someone you trust—a coach, teammate, or captain—you can talk to about it? Open communication is key. What about starting a conversation with a few teammates and then going, together, to the coach? Hagobian also recommends focusing on what you can control and letting go of what you cannot. "In most cases, what you can control is not the situation but how you respond to it." Think: your attitude, your effort, your focus. Ask yourself if your own actions are helping you or the situation. If not, reassess and try again.

Take a team-building retreat. Running camps create the perfect environment to bond with your teammates. Away from distractions at home, in beautiful and sometimes challenging environments, summertime running camps are memory-building, lung-boosting opportunities to learn, explore, and grow.

WRITING PROMPTS

One time I trusted my gut

Who do I want on my support crew?

When I have questions, I ask

If I'm struggling or have an issue, I turn to

11

GEARING UP

THE BASICS AND THE EXTRAS

You don't need a whole lot to run. That's the beauty of running: it's simple. The multibillion-dollar running gear industry might not tell you this, but the only equipment you *really* need is your body. The rest is icing on the cake.

Realistically, though, unless you live in a nudist community, you're going to want to wear clothes. And while you could run barefoot, we recommend running shoes for your comfort and safety. Specific types of shoes are helpful for training and racing, but to start, about any pair of running sneakers will do.

Not so long ago, a runner's gear list included just a few simple items: shoes, cotton tee, cotton socks, regular bra, and shorts. Maybe a hoodie. Runners didn't have GPS watches; waterproof, breathable materials; or goo-filled nutrition packets. Today, newfangled technology changes the game when it comes to comfort and convenience. Fabrics, designs, fit, and materials have improved, including far better options for girls and women. Some "must-have" gear is overblown marketing hype, but performance-ready pieces abound.

In this chapter, we'll discuss the gear you need (and do not need) from head to toe, including tips on sizing, fit, and when-to-replace guidelines. We'll cover sports bras, shoes, apparel, accessories, and tech.

SPORTS BRAS

Breasts move: up, down, around. Stacked on our chest muscles, they're jiggly masses of tissue without the support of muscle or bones. Their anatomy includes fascia layers, milk-producing glands, and blood vessels. Depending on their size and shape, breasts may contribute to a forward lean or other postural issues.

No matter their size, breasts wobble and jostle, especially during high-impact activity like running. This may cause some pain, discomfort, or self-consciousness, especially when your breasts are growing and changing.

A sports bra may be the most useful piece of equipment you own. Although sports bras do not stop movement completely, high-support bras have been shown to improve running mechanics. They also combat discomfort, with multiple features depending on breast size, activity type and duration, and garment design.

HISTORY

The modern sports bra was created in 1977 when three women, Linda Miller, Lisa Lindahl, and Polly Palmer-Smith, sewed two jock straps together to form a "jockbra," later named Jogbra. Since then, the sports bra design has been tweaked, refined, and improved.

What makes the perfect sports bra? The jury is still deliberating, but you know it when you feel it. Designers focus on providing support and limiting motion, plus features like covered fasteners to avoid chafing (rubbing that leaves a painful rash) and specific fabrics to promote

Back issues?

If your breasts strain your back or neck, strengthening your upper back muscles may help; try exercises such as supermans, downward dog, and lat pull-downs.

---

breathability. Research continues, and experts have yet to completely crack the code, but they are getting closer. The good news? There are lots of options, and a little bit of chest-dressing education and try-on experiments can go a long way.

FEATURES

Whether you're endowed with AAs or DDs, as a runner, you'll want a sports bra that handles high impact. (That likely means more than a skimpy bralette, no matter how cute.) "Smaller cup sizes will be fine with a simple pullover compression bra; however, those with larger cup sizes need a bra with independent cup and band sizing, and the right level of compression as well as features that allow you to adjust the bra to your body," says Sally Bergesen, founder and CEO of Oiselle, a women's running apparel company.

Here are factors to consider when you're looking for a sports bra.

Band. A strong, comfortable, stretchy, close-fitting wide band that goes around your rib cage is the most supportive element of a bra. It should not ride up, and it definitely shouldn't squeeze your ribs so much that it restricts your breathing. The front section of the band should sit against your breastbone, not your boobs, and the band should ride level around your body.

Straps. Look for wide and/or padded straps. They shouldn't be so tight that they dig into your neck or shoulders, but they shouldn't be so loose that they fall down either. If you feel numbness or tingling in your arms, try looser straps; some models allow you to adjust the straps.

Chest. To cover, hold, and protect your breasts, bras offer compression (tight-fitting material) or encapsulation (cups for each boob). Some bras combine both features for more support. More coverage area (that is, less cleavage showing) usually means less movement of your breasts. As far as fit, if you're bulging around a cup, the bra is too small; if wrinkles or gaps form, it's too big. To ensure a proper fit with encapsulation, scoop each breast up with one hand and then settle it inside the cup.

Underwire. Firm, U-shaped pieces may provide additional support for your breasts. The U should fit under and around each breast, and if you feel it digging in, find a different bra.

Fabric. Sports bras come in a variety of materials, but whatever the bra is made of should be moisture-wicking and breathable. Synthetic options include nylon, spandex, and polyester, while some bras incorporate natural fibers like wool. The material should feel good against your skin and not irritate sensitive areas, in particular your nipples.

Clasps and hooks. Closures should be adjustable and lined to prevent chafing. Start by wearing a bra on the loosest or middle hooks so you can tighten it as the material naturally stretches over time. The classic racerback style, with no open-close features, requires an over-the-head maneuver. Make sure any metal or plastic parts live in a fabric garage or are otherwise away from your skin.

Feel. Comfort is clutch. Chafing, digging, or pinching sucks. Try on new bras at least once a year; especially as your body changes, bra sizing and styles should too.

FIT

Here's how to get an idea of what size to start with:

1. Using flexible measuring tape, measure around your chest—under your arms but above the widest part of your bust. Measure after exhaling or while sitting down. The number (in inches) is your band size if it's even; if it's an odd number, round up. For example, if it's 35, you're a 36.
2. Measure around the widest section of your bust. Note the inches.
3. Measure around your rib cage, just under your breasts. Take note of the inches.
4. Subtract the rib cage measurement (step 3) from your bust measurement (step 2). The answer correlates to a cup size:

3" → **AA**	6" → **C**	9" → **E**
4" → **A**	7" → **D**	10" → **F**
5" → **B**	8" → **DD**	

Some sports bras are sized by band and cup size, others in generic sizes, like "medium." The best way to find a good fit is to try on sports bras. Many local specialty running shops offer free professional fittings, which can dial in your size and style preferences. When you try on a sports bra, run around, and maybe do a little dance, to test it out.

MAKING IT LAST

You can expect a sports bra to last 6 to 12 months. Expiration signs include fraying, fading, sagging, bagginess, loose straps, loose band, and chafing. They're investments, costing upward of $30 to $100, so take good care of them. You can extend the life of your bra by washing it in cold water by hand, or on a gentle cycle, and air drying (dryer heat breaks it down faster). If you're throwing it in the washer, secure any clasps or straps and place it in a mesh lingerie bag first.

RUNNING SHOES

Hundreds of running shoe styles and designs range from low-priced to $250 or more for one specialized pair. Shoe ads promise that their shoes will make you faster, stronger, injury-free. But can a shoe really do all that for you?

PRO TIP

Double up

Pack an extra sports bra or tank with built-in support to change into after practice or racing. This prevents skin irritation and getting chilled from sitting around in a sweat-soaked bra. To change into a fresh bra without flashing anyone, put the new bra on top of the sweaty one, then pull the sweaty one off from underneath. (Some styles make this easier than others.)

The short answer is no. Don't be fooled by gimmicks or slick ads. Big claims, wild colors, and fancy tech aside, the best shoe—and the best fit—for you *isn't* necessarily the one that your favorite athlete wears or that stands out the most. In fact, the style that is best for you could be the least noticeable (in other words, the one that is so comfortable you hardly notice it).

Studies have shown a relationship between the comfort of a shoe and reduced injury risk, so by all means, judge by feel. And not just how the shoe feels when you slide it on, but how it feels when you run. Pay attention to where the shoe bends or creases—any rubbing or stiff parts? How is your heel-to-toe transition? Smooth? Clunky? Springy? Barely there? One runner might prefer a close-to-the ground style, another might find relief in a stiffer, more stable shoe, while another might prefer something cushioned with lots of bouncy foam. (And everyone should feel fast when they lace up their spikes!)

The goal is to find a shoe that serves a specific purpose (race, track workout, long run on trails) with comfort and the least amount of shoe needed, as Jonathan Beverly explains in his book *Your Best Stride*. The lighter the shoe (without sacrificing the support or cushion your feet crave) the better—you'll run more efficiently.

FIT

When it comes to sizing, throw out any number you have in your head. As with bras, shoe sizing varies by brand and style. Focus instead on how your foot fits in a particular pair.

Running shoes aren't everyday shoes; you'll want to aim for a roomier fit, with about a thumb-width of space between the end of your longest toe and the front of the toe box. You should be able to spread your toes out and comfortably flex your foot. Avoid slipping or gaping around the heel and ankle. Your feet swell later in the day, so try on shoes at the end of the day or after a run to make sure you'll have enough room. A proper fit—length, width, and height—means not just helping you avoid blisters, hot spots, and cramping but also allowing your feet to function the way they are designed to!

Since every brand has different volume and models, you'll want to try on several pairs. Notice how each feels in your arch, instep, heel, and underfoot. If possible, enlist the help of a local running store, where employees are familiar with a wide range of shoes and can help you find a good fit. Some in-store technology can even scan your feet and help narrow down choices. Take a jog, do a few strides, or do a treadmill test to see how the shoes feel at different speeds. Good running shoes aren't cheap, so a test-drive is an important step in your investment.

DIFFERENT RUNS, DIFFERENT SHOES

Your stride—the way you run—changes at various speeds. That's a good reason to consider wearing different shoes for different types of runs, if possible. For example, a lighter-weight, closer-to-the-ground style, such as a racing flat or thin-soled trainer, often feels better when running faster paces, while a highly cushioned pair might better suit your long, slow runs.

Let's take a closer look at the options.

Cushioned shoes. Whether squishy or bouncy, cushioning underfoot can feel great under tired feet or on hard concrete and pavement. The research is out on whether extra cushion actually reduces running's impact forces, but depending on the design, cushioned shoes might offer other perks.

Stability shoes. Whether from dense materials along the inside of the shoe or from a wide base, the support provided by these shoes might feel particularly good for those whose strides aren't super-efficient.

Minimal shoes. With low or no cushioning under the foot and a level platform from heel to toe, a less-is-more design mimics running barefoot. But while "natural running" sounds like a good idea, know that running in minimal shoes may stress your Achilles tendon and lower leg, especially if you're not used to them. You should be working on foot and lower leg strength and resilience anyway, but if you want to run in minimal or zero-drop shoes, it's an absolute must.

Trail shoes. With knobs and nubs on the soles and optional features, such as a rock plate, toe bumpers, and weather-resistant materials, these shoes are designed for rough, rocky, technical, or slick conditions. They should be protective and have good traction. Some models may feel like stiff overkill on roads, but lighter, flexible styles are more versatile on many surfaces.

Racing flats. These lightweight, closer-to-the ground shoes are designed with fast running in mind. Ideal for road races from 5K to marathons, flats are also a good option for workouts, whether on the track, pavement, or soft surfaces. Flats have less material than regular training shoes, but more than spikes, and can ease the transition to more aggressive spikes.

Spikes. Spikes are super-lightweight shoes with hard plastic teeth and screw-in spikes. They provide a sensation of propelling you forward with the aim of encouraging faster turnover. They're ideal for cross-country and track races, and some fast workouts. They provide great traction, but check the rules: Some regions don't allow metal spikes, while others practically require them, thanks to supermuddy courses! Don't wait until race day to run in yours. Practice strides then faster workouts in spikes to build up your lower leg strength and avoid calf cramps on race day.

MAKING THEM LAST

Your shoes may last for 300 to 500 miles. Usually, the guts of the shoe wear out before exterior materials, which tend to be more durable. You might notice some aches or pains popping up in your joints or feet when your kicks are expiring. But unlike with milk, a horrible stench does not reveal a shoe's "best-by" date.

To make your shoes last longer, rotate a few pairs at once. Do not put them in the washing machine or dryer, which is a near-certain death. If they need cleaning, hose them down, remove the insoles and laces, stuff them with newspaper, and let them air-dry.

When you are ready to retire a pair, consider giving them to a shoe-recycling program. Most running stores accept used shoes and will recycle or donate them for you.

OTHER ESSENTIALS

Besides a sports bra and running shoes, other helpful gear includes tops, bottoms, and socks. And as with bras and shoes, comfort is key, and fit, fabric, and other design features directly affect comfort level. Technical fabrics, whether synthetic or natural, can help manage moisture by wicking sweat, drying quickly, allowing for breathability, and protecting you from the elements. Some even help fight odor.

Depending on where you run, some fabrics will work better than others. For example, in hot and humid weather, synthetic featherweight and extremely breathable fabrics will perform better than, say, a fuzzy wool long-sleeve. In cooler conditions, layering different types of fabrics creates a system or "kit" that can suit whatever the day throws at you.

SOCKS

Look for technical fabrics and a sport-specific fit. No matter the cut (no-show, ankle, crew), a sock should sit tight on your foot, not bunch or gap, and be breathable and moisture wicking. That will help prevent blisters and hot spots. Some brands offer pairs with left and right socks; others offer styles designed specifically for a female foot. One eternal debate is whether to wear socks with spikes. Elizabeth is team *No Socks* (aka team Thick Callous); Melody is firmly in the sock camp to avoid blisters, which thin, technical socks may prevent.

SHORTS

From booty shorts to basketball shorts, there are countless styles to choose from. What is most important is to choose technical fabrics that feel good against your skin, to help prevent chafing. Nice touches include pockets, reflective hits, and sewn-in briefs (so you don't have to wear underwear if you don't want to).

PANTS

Options include tights of varying length, joggers, and track-style warm-up pants. They can be worn on their own or layered with other bottoms if it's cold. As with all your gear, look for super-comfortable fabrics. Pockets and reflective hits are bonuses, as are adjustability features like zippers and drawstrings. Avoid seams that rub and wider bottoms that might trip you up. Ideally, the fabrics are flexible and allow for a full range of motion.

TANKS AND TEES

From sleek tanks with built-in bras to loose flowing tees and luxurious long-sleeves, the list of top styles goes on and on. What's most important is choosing tops that don't constrict your movement or cause chafing. Thumbholes, reflective hits, flat seams, just-right length (from crop tops to bum-covering shirts), and stench-fighting fabrics are also features worth considering.

WARMER LAYERS

Half-zips are a great go-to for chilly runs and warm-ups; the zip allows you to control your temp with some venting. Lightweight wind-stopping

---

Uniforms

PRO TIP

A school-issued uniform will likely include a singlet (the sleeveless top with your team name), shorts (or buns aka spankies), and warm-ups. Whether they are (or are not) the most stylish or comfortable, there's definitely something special in donning the same colors as your teammates. Treat your uniform with care and wear it proudly.

Less is more

PRO TIP

Avoid overdressing. It takes 5 to 10 minutes
to warm up on a run, but you will, we promise.
Start a little chilly, even on cooler days!

---

shells are also ideal for keeping your core temperature up without creating a swampy, garbage-bag effect. For wet weather, invest in a lightweight, water-resistant but breathable rain jacket. In a downpour, you're going to get wet no matter what you're wearing, but some protection from the elements helps. For the occasional deluge or blizzard, waterproof breathable pants can save your bacon.

ACCESSORIES

These little extras offer big perks:

> A brimmed hat keeps sun off your face and rain out of your eyes. Trucker, biker, mesh, or visor styles all work, with varying degrees of heat trapping, breathability, and style.

> Headbands keep annoying flyaways out of your face. (You can make one out of an old T-shirt sleeve!)

> Gloves/mittens are essential for late cross-country season, winter, and early track season if you run in places with variable seasons and weather. Look for breathable, waterproof, and snot-wiping-soft materials.

> Technical neck gaiters, also known as buffs, are a versatile wrap that can cover your neck or head as well as go around your wrist as a snot-wipe.

TECH

A watch is a helpful tool. A basic running watch with stopwatch, lap, and split features does the trick. At the very least, it's nice to know the duration of a run so you can record time-on-feet in your training log.

If you want to get fancy, GPS watches can tell you your pace, splits, distance, altitude, cadence, heart rate, and even if a storm is coming! But take this data with a grain of salt. Wearable tech is not always accurate or helpful. For example, heart rate monitors can be great guides, but chest-straps can feel uncomfortable (even if they're the most accurate), and some wrist-based monitors have been shown to be inaccurate.

Honestly, seeing all that data can be fun and insightful, but it can also be misleading and distracting. Relying too much on data dumbs down our internal-feedback systems. If you can use a GPS watch some days, such as to keep your easy days easy or to time your splits during a workout, while avoiding complete dependence on it, then great. The best technology around, though? Your brain-body connection. The most important (and reliable) indicator is *you*.

WRITING PROMPTS

My favorite shoes

My favorite running outfit

For practice each day, I bring

ACKNOWLEDGMENTS

Thank you to every one of our athletes, campers, coaches, teammates, mentors, family members, dear friends, and trail sisters along the path who support and inspire our ongoing running journeys.

We're incredibly grateful for our sources, including women who ran before us and researchers asking important questions. You're integral to the new paradigm of girls running, and we thank you for graciously sharing expertise.

In addition to those mentioned within, we'd like to thank Kara Bazzi and Opal Food and Body, Julie McCleery, Georgie Bruinvels and Fitr-Woman, Ladia Albertson-Junkans, Mary Cain, Isabelle Kennedy and the Melody Fairchild Girls Running Camp crew, Angelina Ramos, Maurica Powell, Robyn McGillis, Marie Davis Markham, Chas Davis, Jonathan Marcus, Liz Gill, Jessica Bishop, Nikki Buurma, Leah Kangas, Jae Gruenke, Victoria Jackson, Lindsay Parks Pieper, Dustin Martin, Margo Jennings, Alison Wade, Lindsay Crouse, Tiffany Stewart, Kathryn Ackerman and the Female Athlete Conference, Katherine Rizzone, Julie Steele, Heather Caplan and Lane 9, Rachael Steil, Ava Asher, Kelsie Clausen, Navalayo Osembo-Ombati, Sarah Lesko, Pam Greene, Jena Winger, Sarah Schwald, the Women's Sports Foundation, Tucker Center for Research on

Girls and Women in Sport, Tony Reed, and especially Harland Yriarte and the Steens Mountain Running Camp family.

Thank you to our VeloPress team, including editor Casey Blaine, for bringing us down to earth, and to Sarah Gorecki and Kara Mannix for their guidance.

To our early readers—thanks again!

Melody

Thank you to Glen and Dakota, for making room at our table for this project; to Pete, Lorrie, Diane, and Karla, for the makeshift office spaces, deep listening, and childcare; this would have been impossible without your support. Thanks to my mom and dad, who gave me wings to fly in the first place.

Elizabeth

Thank you to Lauren Fleshman, Marianne Elliott, Wilder Running, and Hugo House for helping me find my voice. Thank you to editors, especially Jonathan Beverly (PodiumRunner) and Doug Binder (DyeStat), for providing outlets. An extra-special thank you to Sarah Pizzo, Kevin O'Rourke, Kent Siebold, and MT Elliott for real talk and instrumental guidance. Thank you to my mom, Barbara Carey, for infinite love. To my cat, Buckley, for emotional support, albeit sporadic. And, most importantly, thank you to my favorite, Andrew Olson, who made this passion project possible.

SELECTED BIBLIOGRAPHY

Chapter 2. Hello, Body!

Gamble, Karen L., Ryan Berry, Stuart J. Frank, and Martin E. Young. "Circadian Clock Control of Endocrine Factors." *Nature Reviews Endocrinology* 10 (2014): 466–475. https://doi.org/10.1038/nrendo.2014.78.

Mountjoy, Margo, Jorunn Kaiander Sundgot-Borgen, Louis M. Burke, Kathryn E. Ackerman, Cheri Blauwet, Naama Constantini, Constance Lebrun, et al. "IOC Consensus Statement on Relative Energy Deficiency in Sport (RED-S): 2018 Update." *British Journal of Sports Medicine* 52, no. 11 (2018): 687–697. https://doi.org/10.1136/bjsports-2018-099193.

Mountjoy, Margo, Jorunn Sundgot-Borgen, Louis Burke, Susan Carter, Naama Constantini, Constance Lebrun, Nanna Meyer, et al. "The IOC Consensus Statement: Beyond the Female Athlete Triad—Relative Energy Deficiency in Sport (RED-S)." *British Journal of Sports Medicine* 48, no. 7 (2014): 491–497. https://doi.org/10.1136/bjsports-2014-093502.

Rosa-Caldwell, Megan E., and Nicholas P. Greene. "Muscle Metabolism and Atrophy: Let's Talk About Sex." *Biology of Sex Differences* 10, no. 1 (August 2019): 43. https://doi.org/10.1186/s13293-019-0257-3.

Chapter 3. Train like a Boss

Arnold, Amanda, Charles A. Thigpen, Paul F. Beattie, Michael J. Kissenberth, and Ellen Shanley. "Overuse Physeal Injuries in Youth Athletes: Risk Factors, Prevention, and Treatment Strategies." *Sports Health* 9, no. 2 (2017): 139–147. https://doi.org/10.1177/1941738117690847.

Blagrove, Richard C., Glyn Howatson, and Philip R. Hayes. "Effects of Strength Training on the Physiological Determinants of Middle- and Long-Distance Running Performance: A Systematic Review." *Sports Medicine* 48, no. 5 (2018): 1117–1149. https://doi.org/10.1007/s40279-017-0835-7.

Bonnar, Daniel, Kate Bartel, Naomi Kakoschke, and Christin Lang. "Sleep Interventions Designed to Improve Athletic Performance and Recovery: A Systematic Review of Current Approaches." *Sports Medicine* 48, no. 3 (March 2018): 683–703. https://doi.org/10.1007/s40279-017-0832-x.

Casado, Arturo, Brian Hanley, Jordan Santos-Concejero, and Luis M. Ruiz-Pérez. "World-Class Long-Distance Running Performances Are Best Predicted by Volume of Easy Runs and Deliberate Practice of Short-Interval and Tempo Runs." *The Journal of Strength and Conditioning Research* (April 20, 2019). https://doi.org/10.1519/JSC.0000000000003176.

Jauhiainen, Susanne, Andrew J. Pohl, Sami Äyrämö, Jukka-Pekka Kauppi, and Reed Ferber. "A Hierarchical Cluster Analysis to Determine Whether Injured Runners Exhibit Similar Kinematic Gait Patterns." *Scandinavian Journal of Medicine & Science in Sports* 30, no. 4 (2020): 732–740. https://doi.org/10.1111/sms.13624.

Menting, Stein G. P., David T. Hendry, Lieke Schiphof-Godart, Marije T. Elferink-Gemser, and Florentine J. Hettinga. "Optimal Development of Youth Athletes Toward Elite Athletic Performance: How to Coach Their Motivation, Plan Exercise Training, and Pace the Race." *Froniers in Sports and Active Living* 20 (August 2019). https://doi.org/10.3389/fspor.2019.00014.

Saw, Anna E., Luana C., Main, and Paul B. Gastin. "Monitoring the Athlete Training Response: Subjective Self-Reported Measures Trump Commonly Used Objective Measures: A Systematic Review." *British Journal of Sports Medicine* 50, no. 5. (2016): 281–291. https://doi.org/10.1136/bjsports-2015-094758.

van der Sluis, Alien, Michel S. Brink, Babette M. Pluim, Evert A. L. M. Verhagen, Marije T. Elferink-Gemser, and Chris Visscher. "Self-Regulatory Skills: Are They Helpful in the Prevention of Overuse Injuries in Talented Tennis Players?" *Scandinavian Journal of Medicine and Science in Sports* 29, no. 7 (2019): 1050–1058. https://doi.org/10.1111/sms.13420.

Walters, Benjamin K., Connor R. Read, and A. Reed Estes. "The Effects of Resistance Training, Overtraining, and Early Specialization on Youth Athlete Injury and Development." *Journal of Sports Medicine and Physical Fitness* 58, no. 9 (2018): 1339–1348. https://doi.org/10.23736/S0022-4707.17.07409-6.

Chapter 4. Adaptations

Rauh, Mitchell J., Adam S. Tenforde, Michelle T. Barrack, Michael D. Rosenthal, and Jeanne F. Nichols. "Associations Between Sport Specialization, Running-Related Injury, and Menstrual Dysfunction Among High School Distance Runners." *Athletic Training and Sports Health Care* 10, no. 6 (2018): 260–269. https://doi.org/10.3928/19425864-20180918-01.

Swinbourne, Richard, Joanna Miller, Daniel Smart, Deborah K. Dulson, and Nicholas Gill. "The Effects of Sleep Extension on Sleep, Performance, Immunity and Physical Stress in Rugby Players." *Sports* 6, no. 2 (2018). https://doi.org/10.3390/sports6020042.

von Rosen, Philip, Anna Frohm, Anders Kottorp, Cecilia Fridén, and Annette Heijen. "Multiple Factors Explain Injury Risk in Adolescent Elite Athletes: Applying a Biopsychosocial Perspective." *Scandanavian Journal of Medicine and Science in Sports* 27, no. 12 (2017): 2059–2069. https://doi.org/10.1111/sms.12855.

Chapter 5. Running with Hormones

Ackerman, Kathryn E., Vibha Singhal, Charumathi Baskaran, Meghan Slattery, Karen Joanie Campoverde Reyes, Alexander Toth, Kamryn T. Eddy, et al. "Oestrogen Replacement Improves Bone Mineral Density in Oligoamenorrhoeic Athletes: A Randomised Clinical Trial." *British Journal of Sports Medicine* 53, no. 4 (2019): 229–236. https://doi.org/10.1136/bjsports-2018-099723.

Adkisson, Eric J., Darren P. Casey, Darren P. Beck, Alvaro N. Gurovich, Jeffery S. Martin, and Randy W. Braith. "Central, Peripheral, and Resistance Arterial Reactivity: Fluctuates During the Phases of the Menstrual Cycle." *Experimental Biology and Medicine* 235, no. 1 (January 2010): 111–118. https://doi.org/10.1258/ebm.2009.009186.

Armour, Mike, Caroline A. Smith, Kylie A. Steel, and Freya Macmillan. "The Effectiveness of Self-Care and Lifestyle Interventions in Primary Dysmenorrhea: A Systematic Review and Meta-Analysis." *BMC Complementary and Alternative Medicine* 19, no. 1 (2019): 22. https://doi.org/10.1186/s12906-019-2433-8.

Cutolo, Maurizio, Alberto Sulli, Silvia Capellino, B. Villaggio, P. Montagna, Bruno Seriolo, and Rainer H. Straub. "Sex Hormones Influence on the Immune System: Basic and Clinical Aspects in Autoimmunity." *Lupus* 13, no. 9 (2004): 635–638. https://doi.org/10.1191/0961203304lu1094oa.

Draper, C. F., K. Duisters, B. Weger, A. Chakrabarti, A. C. Harms, L. Brennan, T. Hankemeier, et al. "Menstrual Cycle Rhythmicity: Metabolic Patterns in Healthy Women." *Scientific Reports* 8, no. 1 (2018): 14568. https://doi.org/10.1038/s41598-018-32647-0.

Gold, Ellen B., Craig Wells, and Marianne O'Neill Rasor. "The Association of Inflammation with Premenstrual Symptoms." *Journal of Women's Health* 25, no. 9 (2016): 865–874. https://doi.org/10.1089/jwh.2015.5529.

Knowles, Olivia E., Brad Aisbett, Luana C. Main, Eric J. Drinkwater, Liliana Orellana, and Séverine Lamon. "Resistance Training and Skeletal Muscle Protein Metabolism in Eumenorrheic Females: Implications for Researchers and Practitioners." *Sports Medicine* 49, no. 11 (2019): 1637–1650. https://doi.org/10.1007/s40279-019-01132-7.

Lee, Haneul, Jerrold Petrofsky, Nirali Shah, Abdulaziz Awali, Karen Shah, Mohammed Alotaibi, and JongEun Yim. "Higher Sweating Rate and Skin Blood Flow During the Luteal Phase of the Menstrual Cycle." *Tohoku Journal of Experimental Medicine* 234, no. 2 (2014): 117–122. https://doi.org/10.1620/tjem.234.117.

Martin, Daniel, Craig Sale, Simon B. Cooper, and Kirsty J. Elliott-Sale. "Period Prevalence and Perceived Side Effects of Hormonal Contraceptive Use and the Menstrual Cycle in Elite Athletes." *International Journal of Sports Physiology and Performance* 13, no. 7 (2018): 926–932. https://doi.org/10.1123/ijspp.2017-0330.

Thompson, Belinda, Ashley Almarjawi, Dean Sculley, and Xanne Janse de Jonge. "The Effect of the Menstrual Cycle and Oral Contraceptives on Acute Responses and Chronic Adaptations to Resistance Training: A Systematic Review of the Literature." *Sports Medicine* 50, no. 1 (2020): 171–185. https://doi.org/10.1007/s40279-019-01219-1.

Tønnessen, Espen, Ida Siobhan Svendsen, Inge Christoffer Olsen, Alte Guttormsen, and Thomas Haugen. "Performance Development in Adolescent Track and Field Athletes According to Age, Sex, and Sport Discipline." *PLOS One* 10, no. 6 (2015). https://doi.org/10.1371/journal.pone.0129014.

Yesildere Saglam, Havva, and Ozlem Orsal. "Effect of Exercise on Premenstrual Symptoms: A Systematic Review." *Complementary Therapies in Medicine* 48 (2020): 102272. https://doi.org/10.1016/j.ctim.2019.102272.

Young, Simon N. "How to Increase Serotonin in the Human Brain Without Drugs." *Journal of Psychiatry and Neuroscience* 32, no. 6 (2007): 394–399. https://www.ncbi.nlm.nih.gov/pmc/articles/PMC2077351/.

Chapter 6. A Winning Mindset

Abrams, Mitch. "The Complexities of Anger for the Female Athlete." Presentation at the Female Athlete Conference at Babson College, Massachusetts, June 2019.

Breines, Juliana G., and Serena Chen. "Self-Compassion Increases Self-Improvement Motivation." *Personality and Social Psychology Bulletin* 38, no. 9 (2012): 1133–1143. https://doi.org/10.1177/0146167212445599.

Grant, Heidi, and Carol S. Dweck. "Clarifying Achievement Goals and Their Impact." *Journal of Personality and Social Psychology* 85, no. 3 (2003): 541–553. https://doi.org/10.1037/0022-3514.85.3.541.

Hölzel, Britta K., James Carmody, Mark Vangel, Christina Congleton, Sita M. Yerramsetti, Tim Gard, and Sara W. Lazar. "Mindfulness Practice Leads to Increases in Regional Brain Gray Matter Density." *Psychiatry Research* 191, no. 1 (2011): 36–43. https://doi.org/10.1016/j.pscychresns.2010.08.006.

Kini, Prathik, Joel Wong, Sydney McInnis, Nicole Gabana, and Joshua W. Brown. "The Effects of Gratitude Expression on Neural Activity." *NeuroImage* 128, no. 1 (2016): 1–10. https://doi.org/10.1016/j.neuroimage.2015.12.040.

Song Juyeon, Sung-il Kim, and Mimi Bong. "Controllability Attribution as a Mediator in the Effect of Mindset on Achievement Goal Adoption Following Failure." *Frontiers in Psychology* 2943, no. 10 (2020). https://doi.org/10.3389/fpsyg.2019.02943.

The Journey of Women's Running: A Timeline

Schulkin, Jay. "Evolutionary Basis of Human Running and Its Impact on Neural Function." *Frontiers in Systems Neuroscience* 10 (2016): 59. https://doi.org/10.3389/fnsys.2016.00059.

Schultz, Jaime, Jean O'Reilly, and Susan K. Cahn, eds. *Women and Sports in the United States: A Documentary Reader*. Hanover, NH: Dartmouth College Press, 2018.

Staurowsky, Ellen J., Nicholas Watanabe, Joseph Cooper, Cheryl Cooky, Nancy Lough, Amanda Paule-Koba, Jennifer Pharr, et al. "Chasing Equity: The Triumphs, Challenges, and Opportunities in Sports for Girls and Women." New York: Women's Sports Foundation, January 15, 2020. https://www.womenssportsfoundation.org/articles_and_report/chasing-equity-the-triumphs-challenges-and-opportunities-in-sports-for-girls-and-women/.

Chapter 7. Compete like a Champion

Deaner, Robert O., Rickey E. Carter, Michael J. Joyner, and Sandra K. Hunter. "Men Are More Likely than Women to Slow in the Marathon." *Medicine & Science in Sports & Exercise* 47, no. 3 (March 2015): 607–616. https://doi.org/10.1249/MSS.0000000000000432.

Hettinga, Florentina J., Andrew M. Edwards, and Brian Hanley. "The Science Behind Competition and Winning in Athletics: Using World-Level Competition Data to Explore Pacing and Tactics." *Frontiers in Sports and Active Living* 1 (August 2019). https://doi.org/10.3389/fspor.2019.00011.

Chapter 8. Fueling for Success

Cialdella-Kam, Lynn, and Nancy Clark. "Diet Trends and Athlete's Health: Unintended Consequences." Presentation at the Female Athlete Conference at Babson College, Massachusetts, June 7, 2019.

Frączek, Barbara, Andrzej Grzelak, and Andrzej Tadesusz Klimek. "Analysis of Daily Energy Expenditure of Elite Athletes in Relation to their Sport, the Measurement Method and Energy Requirement Norms." *Journal of Human Kinetics* 70 (November 2019): 81–92. https://doi.org/10.2478/hukin-2019-0049.

Gerlach, Kristen E., Harold W. Burton, Joan M. Dorn, John J. Leddy, and Peter J. Horvath. "Fat Intake and Injury in Female Runners." *Journal of the International Society of Sports Nutrition* 5, no. 1 (2008). https://doi.org/10.1186/1550-2783-5-1.

Melin, Anna K., Ida A. Heikura, Adam Tenforde, and Margo Mountjoy. "Energy Availability in Athletics: Health, Performance, and Physique." *International Journal of Sport Nutrition and Exercise Metabolism* 29, no. 2 (2019): 152–164. https://doi.org/10.1123/ijsnem.2018-0201.

Trommelen, Jorn, and Luc J. C. van Loon. "Pre-Sleep Protein Ingestion to Improve the Skeletal Muscle Adaptive Response to Exercise Nutrients." *Nutrients* 8, no. 12 (2016): 763. https://doi.org10.3390/nu8120763.

Chapter 9. Food & Body Issues

Ackerman, Katheryn E., Trent Stellingwerff, Kristy J. Elliott-Sale, Amy Baltzell, Mary Cain, Kara Goucher, Lauren Fleshman, and Margo Mountjoy. "#REDS (Relative Energy Deficiency in Sport): Time for a Revolution in Sports Culture and Systems to Improve Athlete Health and Performance." *British Journal of Sports Medicine* 54, no. 7 (2020): 369–370. https://doi.org/10.1136/bjsports-2019 -101926.

Bazzi, Kara. "Creating a Healthy Sports Culture: Facilitating Athletes' Positive Relationship with Food and Body." Presentation at University of Washington, Seattle, Washington, January 2020.

Carson, T. C. "The Culture and Consequences of Low Energy Availability in NCAA DI Female Distance Runners: A Qualitative Investigation." Poster presentation at the Female Athlete Conference, Babson College, Massachusetts, June 2019.

Kantanista, Adam, Agata Glapa, Adrianna Banio, Wiesław Firek, Anna Ingarden, Ewe Malchrowicz-Mośko, Paweł Markiewicz, Katarzyna Płoszaj, Mateusz Ingarden, and Zuzanna Maćkowiak. "Body Image of Highly Trained Female Athletes Engaged in Different Types of Sport." *BioMed Research International* (January 2018). https://doi.org/10.1155/2018/6835751.

Kato, K., S. Jevas, and D. Culpepper. "Body Image Disturbances in NCAA Division I and III Female Athletes." *The Sport Journal* 21 (2011): 2. http://thesportjournal.org/article/body-image -disturbances-in-ncaa-division-i-and-iii-female-athletes/.

Mask, Lisa, and Céline M. Blanchard. "The Effects of 'Thin Ideal' Media on Women's Body Image Concerns and Eating-Related Intentions: The Beneficial Role of an Autonomous Regulation of Eating Behaviors." *Body Image* 8, no. 4 (2011): 357–365. https://doi.org/10.1016/j.bodyim.2011.06.003.

McIntosh-Dalmedo, Sharon, Wendy Nicholls, Tracey Devonport, and Andrew P. Friesen. "Examining the Effects of Sport and Exercise Interventions on Body Image Among Adolescent Girls: A Systematic Review." *Journal of Sport Behavior* 41, no. 3 (Septempber 2018): 245–268. https://wlv .openrepository.com/handle/2436/620820.

Mountjoy, Margo L., Louise M. Burke, Trent Stellingwerff, and Jorunn Sundgot-Borgen. "Relative Energy Deficiency in Sport: The Tip of an Iceberg." *International Journal of Sport Nutrition and Exercise Metabolism* 28, no. 4 (February 2020): 313–315. https://doi.org/10.1123/ijsnem.2018-0149.

Stewart, Tiffany. "The Female Athlete Body Project: Challenges, Opportunities, and Future Directions." Presentation at the Female Athlete Conference at Babson College, Massachusetts, June 2019.

Wilson, Peter. "Death of the Calorie." *The Economist: 1843*, April/May 2019. https://www.1843 magazine.com/features/death-of-the-calorie.

Chapter 10. Building a Great Team

Bazzi, Kara. "A Letter to Coaches." *Lane* 9, July 5, 2018. https://lane9project.org/2018/07/05/a-letter-to-coaches/.

Eys, Mark, and Jeemin Kim. "Team Building and Group Cohesion in the Context of Sport and Performance Pyschology." *Psychology* (June 2017). https://doi.org/10.1093/acrefore/9780190236557.013.186.

Hunt, Melissa G., Rachel Marx, Courtney Lipson, and Jordyn Young. "No More FOMO: Limiting Social Media Decreases Loneliness and Depression." *Journal of Social and Clinical Psychology* 37, no. 10 (2018): 751–768. https://doi.org/10.1521/jscp.2018.37.10.751.

Kroshus, Emily, J. D. DeFreese, and Zachary Y. Kerr. "Collegiate Athletic Trainers' Knowledge of the Female Athlete Triad and Relative Energy Deficiency in Sport." *Journal of Athletic Training* 53, no. 1 (2018): 51–59. https://doi.org/10.4085/1062-6050-52.11.29.

Mills, Jennifer S., Sarah Musto, Lindsay Williams, and Marika Tiggemann. "'Selfie' Harm: Effects on Mood and Body Image in Young Women." *Body Image* 27 (2018): 86–92. https://doi.org/10.1016/j.bodyim.2018.08.007.

Warner, Anna G., Katherine H. Rizzone, Scott Davis, Timothy Harvey, and Robert D. Chetlin. "Awareness of the Female Athlete Triad in NCAA Cross Country Coaches." *Medicine & Science in Sports & Exercise* 51, no. 6 (2019): 170. https://doi.org/10.1249/01.mss.0000561014.34161.f9.

Chapter 11. Gearing Up

Milligan, Alexandra, Chris Mills, Jo Corbett, and Joanna Scurr. "The Influence of Breast Support on Torso, Pelvis, and Arm Kinematics During a Five Kilometer Treadmill Run." *Human Movement Science* 42 (August 2015): 246–260. https://doi.org/10.1016/j.humov.2015.05.008.

Nigg, Benno M., Jennifer Baltich, Stefan Hoerzer, and Hendrik Enders. "Running Shoes and Running Injuries: Mythbusting and a Proposal for Two New Paradigms: 'Preferred Movement Path' and 'Comfort Filter.'" *British Journal of Sports Medicine* 49, no. 20 (2015): 1290–1294. https://doi.org/10.1136/bjsports-2015-095054.

Rizzone, Katherine. "Does it Fit? Sports Bras and the Female Athlete." Presentation at the Female Athlete Conference at Babson College, Massachusetts, June 2019.

ABOUT THE AUTHORS

Melody Fairchild is a top runner and coach. In high school, she ran cross country and track, winning multiple state and national titles and setting national records, which stood for more than twenty years. She won the 1990 national cross-country championship, setting a course record that still stands, and earned bronze at the World Junior Cross Country Championships in 1991. On the track, Melody was the first American girl to break 10 minutes in the two-mile. After high school, she was an All-American and NCAA champion runner at the University of Oregon. She went on to earn world-class achievements as a pro runner, including competing at the US Olympic Trials and the World Mountain Running Championships, where Team USA took gold. Today, Melody is an elite masters runner and coach. She has served three times as a coach for Team USA, twice for the World Cross Country Championships. In 2007, she created the Melody Fairchild Girls Running Camp to nurture a lifetime of happy, healthy running. She also founded Boulder Mountain Warriors, a youth running club. With more than 20 years of experience in public speaking, Melody presents at running camps and events across the country.

Elizabeth Carey is a writer and running coach. Her work has been published by the *New York Times*, *Runner's World*, *Trail Runner*, *Podium-Runner*, *DyeStat*, and *Outside*. Her running journey started in 1999 on the Cleveland High School track team in Oregon. She ran Division I cross country and track for Columbia University and has coached at all levels of the sport. She explores trail and ultra-running in Seattle, Washington, where she lives with her husband.

VISIT
VELOPRESS.COM

for more on running, cycling, triathlon,
swimming, ultrarunning,
yoga, recovery, mental training,
health and fitness, nutrition, and diet.

SAVE $10
ON YOUR FIRST ORDER

Shop with us and use coupon code
VPFIRST during checkout.